ny:
Close enc th
the Son of God

Jonathan Stephen

DayOne

First printed 1998

All scripture quotations are from The New International Version © 1973, 1978, 1984, International Bible Society. Published by Hodder and Stoughton.

British Library Cataloguing in Publication Data available
ISBN 0 902548 78 6

Published by Day One Publications
3 Epsom Business Park, Kiln Lane, Epsom, Surrey KT17 1JF.
☎ 01372 728 300 **FAX** 01372 722 400
e-mail address: ldos.dayone@ukonline.co.uk

Designed by Steve Devane and printed by Clifford Frost Ltd, Wimbledon SW19 2SE

Dedication

To the congregation of Carey Baptist Church who first heard these sermons preached – and especially to Theodore Bendor-Samuel, a prince in Israel, whom I have been privileged to call my friend.

Foreword

Many Christians, especially new believers, think of the Old Testament as only a document of historic interest. They find the Psalms a blessing, and they know that some of the narrative sections of the books of Samuel and Kings have good moral teaching in them, but they see little in the Old Testament to help them in their spiritual 'walk with Jesus'. Such people will discover from these pages that the Lord Jesus Christ is very clearly displayed in the book of Genesis as he appears to various of the patriarchs.

Jonathan Stephen has in fact done all of us a great service in writing this volume. It will not merely help those believers who, at present, see little value in the Old Testament, it will also be a great strength to all those who have known and valued the Word of God for many years and who seek to live their lives in the light of it.

The author's easy - to-read style and up-to-date application of the truth of God will bring enrichment to many people. This book is greatly enhanced because these chapters started life as sermons preached to several hundred living Christians who were seeking help to cope with the demanding burdens of life. Although they are available on tape, the publishers are to be commended for making this warm teaching available to a much wider audience in the more easily accessible form of a book. This means that many more people will now be able to benefit from theses clear and timely words.

Michael Bentley

Bracknell

February 1998

INTRODUCTION **6**

ACKNOWLEDGEMENTS **7**

1 OUR GLORIOUS PROSPECT **8**

2 THE TAILOR IN THE GARDEN (GENESIS 2 AND 3) **19**

3 WHAT FAITH MUST LIVE WITH AND WITHOUT (GENESIS 12:1-9) **32**

4 TWO SIMPLE QUESTIONS (GENESIS 15) **45**

5 THE GOD WHO SEES ME (GENESIS 16) **57**

6 SHOCK TREATMENT (GENESIS 17) **71**

7 A FAITH RESTORED (GENESIS 18:1-15) **82**

8 PLEADING FOR SODOM (GENESIS 18:16-23) **94**

9 HOMEWARD BOUND (GENESIS 26) **105**

10 STAIRWAY TO HEAVEN (GENESIS 28:10-22) **120**

11 WRESTLING WITH GOD (GENESIS 32:22-32) **133**

12 REFORMATION IN THE FAMILY (GENESIS 35:1-15) **145**

In warmly recommending Dr Hawker's *Poor Man's Commentary*, C H Spurgeon remarks, 'He had no critical capacity, and no ability whatever as an interpreter of the letter; but *he sees Jesus*, and that is a sacred gift which is most precious whether the owner be a critic or no.' So you see I have my defence ready! Spurgeon goes on to say, 'It is to be confessed that he occasionally sees Jesus where Jesus is not legitimately to be seen.' I do not believe I am guilty of that in this volume. In any case, these days the opposite vice is far more prevalent. Modern commentators seem loath to find Jesus anywhere in the Old Testament, even in the clearest of Messianic prophecies.

The truth is that the Old Testament is full of Christ. As Jesus remarked to the unbelieving Jews, 'These are the Scriptures that testify about me' (John 5:39). Little wonder that the hearts of the disciples on the Emmaus road burned within them as, 'Beginning with Moses and all the prophets, he explained to them what was said in all the Scriptures concerning himself' (Luke 24:27). I like to believe that much of what Christ had to say to them was taken up with theophanies! It is so evident that the Son of God loved to anticipate his incarnation by his numerous appearances in human form that he could hardly have failed to dwell on them.

I have adopted a fairly strict definition of theophany in the chapters that follow. I only cover those Bible passages where an appearance of God to human eyes is either explicitly stated or necessarily implied. More detailed reasons are sometimes given as to why a particular episode has been excluded. Nearly half the theophanies of the Bible are to be found in the Book of Genesis and my aim has been to tackle them all. As it is impossible to understand what is going on without filling in the gaps in the narrative, this results, from chapter 3 onwards, in a basic history of the patriarchs.

Little attempt has been made to disguise the fact that the contents of this book began life as a series of sermons. The spiritual applications are therefore frequently direct and personal. My prayer is that they will prove a challenge and a blessing to many. May these appearances of the Saviour to the saints of old make the saints of the present long for the day when they too will see him 'face to face' (1 Corinthians 13:12).

Acknowledgements

I would like to express my grateful thanks to Christine Bazely, without whose remarkable keyboard skills and stoical acceptance of strange working procedures this book would never have seen the light of day. Sheila and Jeremy also deserve a mention, but only they know why, and they are not telling!

Chapter 1

Our glorious prospect

There is a great goal towards which the whole of history is moving. Ever since the fall of man resulted in paradise lost, the great Sustainer of the universe has been plotting a course towards paradise regained. At that time, says the apostle Peter, God shall 'restore everything as he promised long ago through his holy prophets' (Acts 3:21).

It is easy to underestimate grossly the effects of the entry of sin into the universe. When God gazed at his creation at the end of the Sixth Day, it was his glory, his pride and joy. It was 'very good' (Genesis 1:31). But then man, the apex of God's creative genius, fell into sin and the catastrophic consequences extended throughout the cosmos. The harmony of the created order was shattered. Now 'even the heavens are not pure' in the eyes of God (Job 15:15). The 'whole creation', says Paul, has been 'subjected to frustration'. It is in 'bondage to decay' and 'groaning as in the pains of childbirth right up to the present time' (Romans 8:20-22).

How can anyone think lightly of sin when we know that because of it the entire universe is in a state of dislocation and disarray? There is, at present, no peace or harmony between the Creator and his creation; no peace or harmony within the creation itself. But such a disastrous state of affairs will not be permitted to continue indefinitely.

One day there will be ushered in 'a new heaven and a new earth, the home of righteousness' (2 Peter 3:13). Everything will be put right — and all through the atoning death of our Lord and Saviour Jesus Christ! 'Our God was pleased to have all his fulness dwell in him, and through him to reconcile to himself all things, whether things on earth or things in heaven, by making peace through his blood, shed on the cross' (Colossians 1:19-20). Then 'the times will have reached their fulfilment' and 'all things in heaven and on earth' will have been brought 'together under one head, even Christ' (Ephesians 1:10).

A fundamental longing

Most astonishing of all, however, is that the greatest longing in the heart of God is for the restoration of the cause of all the chaos, humanity itself. For this, he is not prepared to wait. The fact is, when Adam sinned, the Lord God lost a great joy which tragically had been so short-lived. With this creature he had made in his own image, he had been able to walk 'in the garden in the cool of the day' (Genesis 3:8) and share sublime fellowship.

But man's sin forced the Lord God to surround himself with 'clouds and thick darkness' (Psalm 97:2). That is why, in our natural state, we now have only the dimmest awareness that there is a God at all and cannot even imagine the divine fellowship for which we were created.

The Lord did not conceal himself simply as an act of judgement. We might say he surrounded himself with clouds and thick darkness for mutual protection. On the one hand, the Lord's eyes are 'too pure to look upon evil' (Habakkuk 1:13) and on the other, man's eyes were now too evil to look on God's purity and live (Exodus 33:20). Yet the Lord always regretted the necessity of having to adopt such a desperate measure. His great desire was to be able once again to look on his creatures in a way that would bring him pleasure and joy.

For man's part, he still has eternity set in his heart (Ecclesiastes 3:11) and a vague perception that something awesome and vital is missing. Whenever the Holy Spirit begins to contend with him, he slowly comes to realise what that 'something' is. He maybe cannot explain it but in truth he is experiencing the most fundamental longing of the human heart—the longing to *see God*. There is no more basic human need than this. We were created to enjoy 'face to face' communion with our Maker and nothing less can ultimately satisfy us. It should therefore be a cause of immense relief and thanksgiving that, despite our sin, there is also still nothing less that will satisfy *him*.

The Book of Job is among the most ancient writings in the Old Testament. Yet even way back, perhaps in days before Israel became a nation, he was able to declare, 'I know that my Redeemer lives, and that in the end he will stand upon the earth. And after my skin has been destroyed, yet in my flesh I will see God; I myself will see him with my own eyes — I, and not another' (Job 19:25-27). He keeps on turning the truth over in his mind. He cannot get over it! What a glorious thing — he is going to see God with his own eyes, after he has died. I do not know how much he understood about the resurrection body, but it must have been a lot more than Old Testament characters are supposed to know about it. He says that after he has died and his flesh has decayed, with his own eyes he is going to see God! But your flesh has decayed! You just said it Job. 'Well, I don't know how it is going to happen', replies the man of God, who is perfectly used to dealing with fallacious arguments, 'There must be a resurrection body, I suppose. All I know is that one day I am going to stand on the earth with my Saviour God and I shall gaze on him with my own eyes.' It was his greatest boast. No wonder he adds, 'How my heart yearns within me!' (Job 19:27).

Here is one of the earliest of Bible heroes experiencing the most fundamental longing of the human heart. This is no new thing. This is not just a Christian hope in the narrowest sense of the word 'Christian'. This has been the longing of countless men and women ever since the Lord first wrapped himself in 'clouds and thick darkness'. Whenever human spirits have been touched by the Spirit of God and they have been to some extent enlightened, then their basic desire, however poorly understood or expressed, is to see God.

King David put it most clearly, when he prayed in the Psalms, 'And I — in righteousness I shall see your face; when I awake, I shall be satisfied with seeing your likeness' (Psalm 17:15).

As we would expect, the same fundamental longing is many times reflected in the New Testament. As Paul puts it in 1 Corinthians 13: 'Now we see but a poor reflection as in a mirror; then we shall see face to face' (verse 12). The apostle has reached the great culmination of his wonderful chapter on love, which he declares to be the greatest thing of all. It is as though Paul says, 'And who is the personification of this love? Who is the source and who must be its object? Why, the Lord Jesus Christ, of course! And do you not want to *see* the one you love? Of course you do! Why, that is the ultimate fulfilment of this love. The great consummation of the marriage between Christ and his church will come when the bride feasts her eyes on the Lamb.'

No matter how much we may come to know upon this earth it can still only be like a 'poor reflection' of the glorious reality. We could bear no more. It is like when there is an eclipse of the sun and everyone is advised, as they always are, 'Don't look at the sun directly. Just put a pinhole through a piece of card and see the reflection.' As far as the glorified Christ is concerned, a reflection is all we can see as poor, fragile sinners here upon the earth. 'But', says Paul, 'I am looking forward to that day when I shall see him face to face.' That is the great and glorious prospect that awaits 'all who have longed for his appearing' (2 Timothy 4:8).

Do you not sense something of this yearning stirring in your own soul? Is this not what you want more than anything else? Does it not put everything else into perspective in your life and mine, not least all the little moans and groans we have about all sorts of matters? There is little danger of my getting things out of proportion when I keep in the forefront of my mind the fact that one day I shall see my Saviour. What does it really matter what next week brings, or next year? I shall see God! And that is the great longing of my heart.

If that is truly the case with us, we may encourage ourselves with the knowledge that we cannot long for such communion as much as our Lord does. And he will make it happen! 'Blessed are the pure in heart,' said Jesus, 'for they will see God' (Matthew 5:8). There is the Saviour's own promise to us. Anne Ross Cousin's most famous hymn, 'The sands of time are sinking' puts it beautifully:

The bride eyes not her garment,
But her dear bridegroom's face;
I will not gaze at glory,
But on my King of grace;
Not at the crown he giveth,
But on his piercèd hand:
The Lamb is all the glory
Of Immanuel's land.

There is another hymn that we often sing which states, 'Our God is the end of the journey'.[1] I can truly think of no other subject than the one before us in this book which would better help us to keep that simple objective in view or would better prepare us for that glorious prospect.

The Angel of the Lord

In the following chapters, we are going to be looking at those episodes in the Scripture when it seems that the Lord could not wait for time to run its course—those occasions when, in a sense, the future broke through into history and the Lord revealed himself to the eyes of a select number of highly favoured men and women. Our subject is 'theophany', a word which refers to those startling appearances of God which inevitably changed for ever the lives of those who witnessed them.

Theophanies occur throughout the biblical record but nearly half of them are to be found in the Book of Genesis. The reason for this lies most probably in the necessity of establishing early the true nature of God in the minds of his chosen people. No more vivid, immediate and personal means of doing this could be imagined. As we plot our course through Genesis by way of these theophanies, not only shall we find ourselves constantly reminded of 'the end of the journey', we shall also derive tremendous practical assistance to help and strengthen us along the way. We shall discover that the Lord revealed himself in many different ways, and for many different purposes.

Yet, without exception, he did so at moments of critical importance in the lives of those who saw him, moments with which all of us are able readily to identify. They are moments of great crisis, of great need, of great joy, of great uncertainty — those significant moments that all of us experience as we go through life.

In the theophanies of the Bible the Lord appears in a variety of forms. As far as we are concerned in Genesis we shall find that the Lord comes most frequently in the guise of the Angel of the Lord. Usually this guise appears so human that initially he is not even recognised for who he is. It is only later on, as the miracle unfolds, that the recipient of the theophany suddenly realises, usually with terror, who it is that he or she is dealing with.

As the centuries pass, God appears to his people in less material forms. He comes now in the dreams and the visions of his prophets. These appearances are often so 'unveiled', that they completely overwhelm the godly, though of course still sinful, men to whom they are granted.

Nonetheless, however he comes, the Lord always appears with merciful and loving intentions. As one commentator has put it, 'He graciously adopted such methods to indicate how much he longed for the fulness of time when he should put away their sins and bring in an everlasting righteousness for them.'[2] In these theophanies, the Lord indicates just how much he wants to be with his people.

A seeming paradox

Perhaps enough has been said at this stage to provoke the question, 'But how could God do this? How could God actually appear to man?' Have we not already seen God cannot look on man and man cannot look on God? Does not the apostle Paul speak of 'God the blessed and only Ruler, the King of kings and Lord of lords, who alone is immortal and who lives in unapproachable light, *whom no one has seen or can see*' (1 Timothy 6:15,16)? And surely John writes, 'No one has *ever* seen God' (1 John 4:12). Obviously we have to deal with this question before we can continue. Otherwise it will nag away at us and cause all kinds of confusion. The answer lies at the very heart of the Christian faith. It *is* impossible for sinners and an unveiled, holy God to co-exist in close proximity. But the gospel reveals the solution. There is a 'mediator between God and men, the man Christ Jesus' (1 Timothy 2:5). If God can appear to man at all, it must therefore be in the Person of the Son. This is not simply a theological deduction. As we shall see, all the evidence of Scripture confirms that it is so.

In the Hebrews 11 hall of fame, we read that Moses 'regarded disgrace for the sake of Christ as of greater value than the treasures of Egypt, because he was looking ahead to his reward. By faith he left Egypt, not fearing the king's anger; he persevered because *he saw him who is invisible*' (verses 26-27). We seem now to have encountered another problem! 'He saw him who is invisible.' What does the writer mean by that? The whole account is extremely helpful to us. Although commentators on this passage generally fail to notice the connection, it seems to me we have a clear reference here to the theophany at the burning bush (Exodus 3 and 4). This dramatic and well-known episode constitutes Moses' call to deliver the nation of Israel from Egypt. For the purpose, the Lord appears to Moses in the flames of a burning bush which is not consumed. Forty years previously, Moses had 'fled from Pharaoh' (Exodus 2:15), afraid for his life. Far away in Midian he had then hidden himself away, married, raised a family and was quietly living the life of a shepherd. Then the Lord appeared to him in the burning bush. In probably less than an hour, he is transformed from being a retiring, resentful man, still bristling from his previous rejection by the Israelites, into the potential leader of God's people. It was at the burning bush that Moses' life and destiny were radically redirected. It was there, as a result of a theophany, that he was turned from fear to faith.

But notice what it was that caused Moses to leave his settled security for the uncertainty and danger that he knew lay ahead. He gave up everything, says the writer to the Hebrews, '*for the sake of Christ*'. Moses gave up everything not just 'for God'. He gave it up 'for the sake of Christ'. Why? Because it was Christ who met him in the burning bush. It was Christ who challenged, exhorted, rebuked and commissioned him there. Moses owed his 'conversion' to Christ. In other words, it was in the Lord Jesus Christ that Moses 'saw him who is invisible'.

It is the apostle John who explains this seeming paradox to us most explicitly. Because, of the four Gospel writers, John is the most determined to highlight the divinity of Jesus, he sees the need to clear up the dilemma before us straight away. 'No one has ever seen God, but God the One and Only, who is at the Father's side, has made him known' (John 1:18). We see 'the glory of God in the face of Christ' (2 Corinthians 4:6). Jesus himself declared, 'When (a believer) looks at me, he sees the one who sent me' (John 12:45). No wonder he is so distressed when, as late as that final Passover meal, Philip can say, 'Lord, show us the Father and that will be enough for us.' And we read, 'Jesus answered, "Don't you know *me*, Philip, even after I have been among you such a long time? *Anyone who has seen me has seen the Father*. How can you say, 'Show us the Father?'"' (John 14:8-9).

Shekinah glory

Here, of course, is one of the fundamental points that the apostle John is seeking to get across in his Gospel. He could say, 'We have seen his glory, the glory of the One and Only' (John 1:14). In the first half of that verse, John tells us that in Jesus, 'The Word became flesh and made his dwelling (literally "tabernacled") among us'. We know that in the original tabernacle there was the ark of the covenant and upon the atonement cover, or 'mercy seat', there rested the Shekinah glory, the visible presence of God among his people.

But then the apostle says, 'Look, we have seen Jesus' glory and I am telling you, it is *the* glory, it is the Shekinah glory.' This visible representation of God's presence had long since departed. The ark itself had been lost over 600 years before John first looked on Jesus. That had been a result of God's judgement. But now God had tabernacled once again with his people in the Person of the Lord Jesus Christ. 'We have seen his glory, *the* glory of the One and Only, who came from the Father, full of grace and truth.' According to John, whenever the Lord Jesus Christ performed a miracle, he 'revealed his glory' to those who watched with the eye of faith (John 2:11).

And so we find our way to the great statements of the New Testament letters. Listen to Paul writing to the Corinthians: 'The god of this age has blinded the minds of unbelievers, so that they cannot see the light of the gospel of the glory of Christ, who is the image of God' (2 Corinthians 4:4). This reinforces what we have seen so far. Without the eye of faith we cannot see the glory of Christ. This glory is the Shekinah glory because Jesus is the image of God.

As Paul says directly when he writes to the Colossians, 'He is the image of the invisible God,' (Colossians 1:15). Will we ever see God? Yes, in the face of Jesus Christ. In any other way? No; in the face of Jesus Christ. The Second Person of the Trinity is 'the image of the invisible God'. Or as the writer to the Hebrews puts it, 'The Son is the radiance of God's glory and the exact representation of his being,' (1:3).

I shall have more to say on the vital point of Christ as the image of God in the next chapter. All we need to grasp at this stage is that when God reveals himself in Scripture to the eyes of man, he reveals himself through the Son.

The preincarnate Christ

We can demonstrate this truth in another way. In virtually all the early theophanies, as has already been stated, God appears as the Angel of the Lord. Who is this Angel of the Lord? Well, in the very last reference to him in the Old Testament, Malachi declares that this Angel, this messenger of the covenant, is none other than 'the Lord' who 'will come to his temple' (3:1). And the New Testament tells us that this prophecy is fulfilled in Christ (Mark 1:2). So the Bible teaches that theophanies involving the Angel of the Lord are appearances of the Second Person of the Trinity, the Son of God, the Lord Jesus Christ.

Similarly, if we look at the later theophanies, when God appears most frequently in awesome visions, we are again persuaded, on scriptural evidence, that it is the Son who is seen. Consider the first and probably the most celebrated of them, when the Lord appears to the prophet Isaiah. You remember his dramatic description: 'In the year that King Uzziah died, I saw the Lord seated on a throne, high and exalted, and the train of his robe filled the temple . . . "Woe to me!" I cried. "I am ruined! For I am a man of unclean lips, and I live among a people of unclean lips, and my eyes have seen the King, the Lord Almighty"' (6:1,5). Here is an undoubted theophany. 'My eyes have seen the King, the Lord Almighty.' And what is the apostle John's comment? 'Isaiah said this because he saw Jesus' glory and spoke about him,' (John 12:41). Quoting the passage from Isaiah, John says it was Jesus that Isaiah saw in that great and lofty vision.

So whether we are dealing with the earlier or later theophanies, we are dealing with appearances of Christ, close encounters with the Son of God. This is the only conclusion that the Bible consistently offers.

'The Word became flesh' at the incarnation. The Word never became flesh before Jesus was born into the world two thousand years ago. Yet the Lord Jesus Christ appeared on earth before that many times, and often in a very tangible, human form. These theophanies are sometimes called 'Christophanies', to highlight this truth. However, we shall stay with the more common term and so avoid the possibility of planting the idea that there might be theophanies that are not Christophanies!

Understanding that all the theophanies were preincarnate appearances of our Saviour provides fresh and powerful insight into his love for humanity. He so wanted to be with his people, he could not wait for the time to 'fully come' (Galatians 4:4) when he would be born into the world. So he came again and again! (You may be surprised to discover how many theophanies there are.) He wanted to come in order to be with his people, to assure them of his love, to be with those for whom he would eventually suffer and die. So the theophanies were a preparation for his first coming but, as we started out by saying, they prepare *us* for his return.

If we are among those who 'eagerly wait for our Lord Jesus Christ to be revealed' (1 Corinthians 1:7), if we identify with those who 'wait for the blessed hope — the glorious appearing of our great God and Saviour Jesus Christ' (Titus 2:13), then we shall surely be those who long to understand why and how he appeared before. And as we study these divine visitations we shall not only increase in understanding, we shall truly learn to long for his appearing.

In his great high priestly prayer in John 17, Jesus closes with the most ambitious of all his requests: 'Father, I want those you have given me to be with me where I am, and to see my glory' (verse 24). Notice he does not say, 'Father, I want them to be with me where I am, to see *your* glory,' because that would be wrong theologically, we might say, wrong theophanically! He says, 'I want them to be with me to see *my* glory.' That prayer, of course, will most certainly be answered.

Does not every true Christian thrill to these words in John's first letter? 'Dear friends, now we are children of God, and what we will be has not yet been made known. But we know that when he appears, we shall be like him, for we shall see him as he is."(3:2). When the Lord Jesus appears we shall see him *as he is*. Just as it was Jesus that those favoured few saw in the theophanies recorded in the Scriptures, so it is that same Jesus that we shall see 'face to face' when the ultimate communion with God, for which we were created, is finally restored.

Do you recall some of the very last words in the whole Bible? 'The throne of God and of the Lamb will be in the city, and his servants will serve him. They will see his face, and his name will be on their foreheads' (Revelation 22:3-4). How wonderfully and repeatedly the believer is reassured that his most fundamental need, to see God, will be met in glory.

But before going beyond this introductory chapter, let us remember an apt warning we can easily ignore: 'without holiness, no one will see the Lord' (Hebrews 12:14). No one will see Jesus in glory who has not first seen Jesus spiritually here on earth with the eye of faith. But never let us become complacent, relying on a profession we made years ago. We dare not expect to gaze on Christ in the age to come if we do not daily 'fix our eyes on Jesus' now (Hebrews 12:2).

Notes

1 **William Vernon Higham,** *'I saw a new vision of Jesus'.*

2 **A W Pink,** *Gleanings in Joshua,* Moody Press, p. 143.

The tailor in the garden

Genesis 2-3

Old Testament believers were right to wonder how they could look on God and live.[1] They would have readily agreed with the words of the hymn: 'Immortal, *invisible*, God only wise, in light *inaccessible*, hid from our eyes.'[2] But, understanding something of the unique ministry of the Lord Jesus Christ, the New Testament believer may confidently sing, 'Thou art the everlasting Word, the Father's only Son; *God manifestly seen* and heard, and heaven's beloved one.'[3] With great joy he has begun to realise how his fundamental longing one day to 'see God' can and will be satisfied. Moreover, he begins to appreciate why that longing is there in his heart in the first place.

Though the image of God within him has been horribly defaced by sin, the Father has 'predestined' him to be once more 'conformed to the likeness of his Son' (Romans 8:29). With that end in view, he has been given a 'new self, *created to be like God* in true righteousness and holiness' (Ephesians 4:24). By God's grace and the power of the indwelling Holy Spirit, the Christian trusts that he is 'being transformed into his likeness with ever-increasing glory' (2 Corinthians 3:18) even in this life. But he recognises that the completion of the work cannot occur until he *sees God*. The apostle John explains: 'Dear friends, now we are children of God, and what we will be has not yet been made known. But we know that when he appears, we shall be like him, for we shall see him as he is' (1 John 3:2).

This verse refers not to the time when the soul of the believer enters heaven at death but to that great day when Christ will return to preside over the renewal of the universe. Not until then can we be completely conformed to his likeness, for it is not until that day of resurrection that he 'will transform our lowly bodies so that they will be like his glorious body' (Philippians 3:21). Only, says Paul, when we have received our glorified bodies, shall we finally 'bear the likeness of the man from heaven' (1 Corinthians 15:49). Then we shall be truly 'like him, for [along with Job, with our "own eyes"] we shall see him as he is.'

We need to explore the relationship between 'the image of God' and theophany a little further before we are ready to come to the Bible's startling first example.

God's image in man

Let us go right back to the creation of man and the fellowship that he enjoyed with God before the fall. In Genesis 1, on the Sixth Day of creation, we read in verses 26 and 27, 'Then God said, "Let us make man in our image, in our likeness, and let them rule over the fish of the sea and the birds of the air, over the livestock, over all the earth, and over all the creatures that move along the ground." So God created man in his own image, in the image of God he created him; male and female he created them.' (Notice, in passing, that 'man' is a generic term. In other words, it refers to all human beings, both male and female.)

For the first time in the Bible, in these verses we read of a conversation within the Godhead. Instead of the usual formulation: 'Let there be light', or 'Let the land produce living creatures' or whatever it might be, what we have here is 'Let *us* make man in *our* image, in *our* likeness.' God the Father, God the Son and God the Holy Spirit cannot help but reflect on the fact that they are about to bring into being their most profound, most complex and most wonderful creature of all. There is, as it were, a kind of hiatus in the process of creation. It is as though the members of the Godhead pause for a moment's reflection before saying, 'Now for it! Let us make man in our image, in our likeness.' Man is the crown of God's creation, because he alone has been made in God's image and God's likeness, so that he might reflect the nature of God and enjoy true fellowship with him.

This is what distinguishes him from the animals. Man was created 'from the dust of the ground' (Genesis 2:7). Our bodies, in common with those of the animals, are formed from the basic elements of the earth. What separates us from them is not a matter of mere chemistry or biology. What makes man different and altogether higher than the animals is that he alone has been made in the image of God. Now this explains not only why the Lord so wants to have fellowship with us but also why, in almost every instance of theophany, the Lord Jesus Christ appears in human form. If I can say it reverently, the Lord Jesus Christ is 'comfortable' in human form and was so *before the incarnation*. Why? Because man was made in his image.

It has often been asserted that the image of God in man refers exclusively to non-physical characteristics. Man is made in God's image because he has an eternal spirit which gives him the ability consciously to worship God. He is gifted with 'self-consciousness'. By that is not meant shyness or the tendency to be easily embarrassed, but rather that man has the power to contemplate himself, to reflect upon his being. He has the capacity to reason. He has been given a conscience, a moral faculty—he can distinguish between good and bad. He can exercise freedom of choice; he can choose what course of action he takes and is not governed by mere instinct. He possesses an appreciation of aesthetic qualities—he is able to recognise and respond appropriately to beauty and harmony. All these things separate him from the animals, and no doubt the list could be considerably extended. Unquestionably, all these spiritual, moral, intellectual and emotional qualities help define the image of God in man. Indeed, the more they are brought in captivity to the obedience of Christ in our lives, the more we reflect that image. We then find that our new self 'is being renewed in knowledge in the image of its Creator' (Colossians 3:10).

The double image

However, as should be clear from what has been said so far, the biblical doctrine of the image of God should not be defined in purely non-physical terms. At this point we can easily slip into an unscriptural dualism. There is what the old commentators used to call 'the double image'[4]. God's image and likeness is also reflected in man's physical body. When Paul said of the incarnate Christ that 'He is the image of the invisible God' (Col. 1:15), that is exactly the point being made. An image has to be visible! We have of course to be careful. 'God is spirit' (John 4:24). Nevertheless, he created a body for man that was designed to reflect much of his true nature.

This is one of the reasons why the human body is a precious thing, not simply, for example, to be discarded at death. This is why the body of an unbeliever, though never 'a temple of the Holy Spirit' (1 Corinthians 6:19) should still be treated with reverence.

In what way is the image of God reflected physically in the human body? Many suggestions have been made. Unlike the animals, human beings have an upright stance. Commentators of old would reflect on the fact that, as a result, men naturally look up rather than down. Less quaint to modern taste, perhaps, is the observation that we have a face capable of expressing the whole gamut of emotions. Uniquely, we can weep. The Lord Jesus himself reflected the heart of God by this means on many occasions.[5]

Most profoundly, of course, the image of God is reflected physically in the faculty of speech. We are capable of communicating and expressing truth in spoken words and of doing so feelingly, from a whisper to a shout. God spoke creation into being and the power of the spoken word in human affairs remains a reflection of that fact. Supremely, the Word of God, when he was made flesh, needed to be able to express himself. Had man's body not been made appropriately, communication would have been impossible.

The Lord created the body of man knowing that it would be suitable for his own incarnation. He was 'made in human likeness' and 'found in appearance as a man' (Philippians 2:7-8). And that incarnation was not just for a moment, but for the whole of eternity. How could Christ have taken upon himself a body that was not itself the image of God, when he was to have that body for ever? It would have been unimaginable. Similarly, believers themselves shall forever possess glorified versions of the bodies they now inhabit. It is beyond belief that the saints shall one day be perfectly conformed to God's image, except in this one respect. In the eternal state, we shall live, according to the Lord's original design, body and soul. We must reject the unbiblical notion that God's image cannot extend to our physical nature. Both body and soul are scarred and defaced by sin, but the image of God should be discerned in both.

No wonder then that, whether as the Angel of the Lord or in the glorious visions of the later prophets, the theophanies reveal Christ in human form. We should not be unduly amazed that God appears in the image and likeness of man when man was made in the image and likeness of God in the first place.

Neither should we therefore find it surprising that the Lord Jesus Christ appeared habitually to Adam and Eve in such a way — before that dreadful sin was committed that persuaded him to surround himself with clouds and thick darkness. Indeed, before that sin occurred, this is exactly what we might expect.

Taking Genesis 3 literally

So we turn for our first theophany to the Garden of Eden. The normal state of affairs in that place before the Fall is probably indicated in Genesis 3:8: 'Then the man and his wife heard the sound of the LORD God as he was walking in the garden in the cool of the day.' They heard the *sound* of the LORD God as he was walking—not the *voice*, as it says in the Authorised Version. They heard the sound of his walking; they heard his footsteps! Now it is amazing how many conservative commentators, who will fight tooth and nail to maintain a *literal* Adam and Eve in a *literal* garden, are anxious to spiritualise away this theophany. Arriving at verse eight they declare, sometimes with obvious embarrassment, 'This language is, of course, anthropomorphic.' In other words, here is God accommodating himself to our limited human understanding. The mention of human characteristics is simply picture language. The Bible speaks of God's eyes, ears, hands, etc., but we are not to take these terms literally. In the same way, we are not to think of God literally walking in the Garden here in Genesis 3.

But the account of the Garden of Eden is given as sober history and is a very dangerous place to start talking about picture language — a very dangerous place indeed. Why stop there? If God himself is referred to in picture language, then why not Satan? There was no real talking 'serpent'. And what then of the fruit, the trees and the Garden itself? And if all is picture language, then Adam and Eve become mere symbolic representations — and then we are really in trouble . . .

Besides, the notion that there is no true theophany here falls apart disastrously by the time you get to verse 21: 'The Lord God made garments of skin for Adam and his wife and clothed them.' Why should God the tailor be any less credible than God the carpenter? As there was nobody else present to make the garments, anthropomorphists are reduced to saying, rather lamely, 'We don't know how these garments were made.' Or worse, they conclude the work must have been done by Adam and Eve themselves, which not only contradicts what is said but completely overthrows the tremendous theological significance of what is happening, as we shall see. No, let us just assume there are no details in the account of our first parents that need to be spiritualised away.

If you have never considered Chapters 2 and 3 of Genesis in this light before, then it is a great place to begin to realise just how vividly practical and challenging to the spiritual life a study of theophany can be. A good policy to adopt when approaching historical narrative in the Scriptures is to project yourself into the situation and imagine you were there. Start asking some questions: 'If I was there, what would I see, what would I hear, what would I feel?'

Let us put ourselves in the place of Adam and Eve. Assuming we are dealing here with the first theophany of the Bible, what did it mean to this first man and woman to see God at work in these various ways — actually to see him, as plainly as their descendants saw the Lord Jesus Christ when he walked the earth in New Testament days? And what should it mean to us, as the same Saviour works in similar ways in our lives, even though the difference is that we do not see him? This is the value of looking at theophany. We say, 'That's how it would be if we saw him and really that is how it is, even though we do not see him.' For example, the impression is given in Genesis 3:8 that Adam and Eve had a regular appointment with the Lord.

How have your 'quiet times' been recently? Imagine a regular evening slot, with the Lord Jesus Christ himself coming to you! How you would long for the sound of his footfall. How eagerly Adam and Eve must have looked forward to that time of fellowship. What questions they must have asked; what answers they would have expected, because the Son of God himself was there!

This is where the theophany sharpens our thinking to the point of realising that the Lord Jesus Christ will meet us just as really and truly in his Word, even though we do not see his approach, and even though we do not gaze at him as he converses with us in the Scripture. With what eager wonder we would await his arrival, conduct him into the living room and open our Bibles together! But the only difference is that he comes to us spiritually rather than physically. Though we do not see him, he is just as truly present. We may ask the same vital questions with the same expectation of reply.

Guidance and freedom

Let us see what happens when we examine the momentous events of Genesis 2 and 3 in this new light. We take up the account immediately after the creation of Adam. 'Now the LORD God had planted a garden in the east, in Eden; and there he put the man he had formed' (Genesis 2:8). Most people believe Adam was created in the Garden of Eden but this verse strongly implies otherwise. God formed Adam on the earth somewhere to the west of Eden, and then apparently led him into the Garden.

What was the point of that? Well, put yourself in Adam's place. With wide-eyed astonishment he is guided through a novel landscape that was pleasant enough. After all, everything God had created was 'very good' (Genesis 1:31). Yet when he eventually entered Eden, upon which the Lord had lavished such special attention, he knew this was the place for him. One purpose of the journey was so that Adam would never dream of thinking that the grass was greener anywhere else. The Lord wanted him to know that the home he had provided for him was the very best place to be.

Now imagine the Lord Jesus Christ had appeared to you and led you through the front door into your house and said, 'This is the home that I have prepared for you.' Think of him doing the same at your place of work. Imagine the Lord taking you by the hand and bringing you into the building where you worship with your fellow-believers and saying, 'Here is the fellowship for you!'

Do you not think we might all be a little more inclined to acknowledge his leading if Christ appeared to us and took us by the hand and brought us into these situations? I am sure we would. No matter what the difficulties or discouragements or temptations to move out might be, we would stay until he clearly led us elsewhere. Well, of course, the lesson is that his guidance is no less sure simply because we do not see him or feel his hand in ours. Further, notice verse 15. 'The Lord God took the man and put him in the Garden to work it and take care of it.' He is saying, 'I have not put you here just to sit down and enjoy my creation, but to work and to take care of it.' This applies to our home, our place of work and to our church. We are stewards of every situation into which God leads us; every place where God says, 'This is where I want you to be.'

Next, Adam receives the liberty of the Garden. It is an indication of our fallen nature that the small prohibition of verse 17 looms larger in our minds than the great concession that precedes it. 'And the LORD God commanded the man, "You are free to eat from any tree in the garden; but you must not eat from the tree of the knowledge of good and evil, for when you eat of it you will surely die."' Fancy receiving an offer like that, straight from the lips of the Lord Jesus! What freedom he gives to Adam! He can eat almost anything he likes in this glorious garden laid out in front of him.

Does God not do the same for us? Does he not give us perfect freedom once we have found forgiveness of sins in the Lord Jesus Christ? Does he not 'provide us with everything for our enjoyment' (1 Timothy 6:17)? But you say you are finding the Christian life something of a drudgery at the moment. What is wrong with you? Has not the Lord Jesus Christ, in effect, with a sweep of his hand, shown you the new life you have entered and declared, 'if the Son sets you free, you will be free indeed' (John 8:36)?

How small was the restriction laid on Adam—just one tree. In the same way, the Lord Jesus puts no great restrictions upon us. I sometimes meet Christians who act as though their faith is a terrible straightjacket! What a miserable business they make the Christian life appear. Satan suggests God said, 'You must not eat from any tree in the garden' (Genesis 3:1), and some Christians seem almost to believe it.

The Saviour's gift of a wife

'Now the LORD God had formed out of the ground all the beasts of the field and all the birds of the air. He brought them to the man to see what he would name them; and whatever the man called each living creature, that was its name' (verse 2:19). Picture the scene. Think in terms of a theophany. The man sees the Lord bringing these animals to him one by one. How did Adam feel as the Son of God personally brought all these creatures to him for naming? Adam had already been told he was to rule them (1:26). Now he begins to do so. Presumably, this process took many hours but every moment of it taught him far more than merely the diversity of God's creation. With every creature the Lord brought to him, Adam grew in the assurance of his uniquely privileged position. He was working alongside the Lord! He was making decisions that the Son of God was prepared to ratify! Slowly, he began to understand the great dignity that had been conferred on him. He was certainly not an animal. With growing awe and humility, the sinless Adam came to realise that he had been designed as the crown of creation for fellowship with God.

Adam is the representative man. What the Lord says to him he says to us. In an age and culture where we are constantly taught that man is merely an animal, we need the assurance this episode conveys. Though the image of God may be horribly defaced, no human being is either to act or be treated as an animal. Christians, in whom the image is being restored, must recognise their inherent dignity and worth and aspire to the high calling of co-labouring with Christ modelled here in Genesis 2:19.

It is at this point that God creates the woman. He had already decided, 'It is not good for the man to be alone. I will make a helper suitable for him' (verse 18). 'So the LORD God caused the man to fall into a deep sleep; and while he was sleeping, he took one of the man's ribs and closed up the place with flesh. Then the LORD God made a woman from the rib he had taken out of the man, *and he brought her to the man*' (verses 21-22). I love this part of the theophany. The Lord Jesus is there with Adam as he sleeps; and he is not idle. Adam wakes and sees the woman. The Son of God takes her by the hand, puts her hand into the hand of the man and says, 'Here is the conmpanion you need. I have made her for you.'

I do not suppose Adam ever doubted it! After all, the Lord had personally brought her to him. You see the value of appreciating the full theophany. Christian husband, have you come to take your wife for granted? Have you sometimes even wondered whether you have married the right woman? Would you have felt that way if the Lord Jesus himself had personally brought her to you, had placed her hand in yours? Yet that is exactly what the Lord Jesus Christ *has* done for you, even though you did not see him. The theophanies of the Bible are there to help us realise just how much Christ has done for us in our lives and to see just how surely, carefully, lovingly and personally he directs us.

After the Fall

It is not part of my purpose to consider the sad details of the Fall of Adam and Eve, except to note the obvious point that it took place when the Lord was absent. When he returns, how terribly different is the relationship.

'Then the man and his wife heard the sound of the LORD God as he was walking in the garden in the cool of the day, and they hid from the LORD God among the trees of the garden. But the LORD God called to the man, "Where are you?" He answered, "I heard you in the garden, and I was afraid because I was naked; and so I hid." And he said, "Who told you that you were naked? Have you eaten from the tree from which I commanded you not to eat?" The man said, "The woman you put here with me — she gave me some fruit from the tree, and I ate it." Then the LORD God said to the woman, "What is this you have done?" The woman said, "The serpent deceived me, and I ate"' (Genesis 3:8-13). Imagine that! Imagine being closely questioned by the Lord Jesus Christ as he asks you this essential spiritual question, 'Where are you?' Would you pass the buck along the line as Adam and Eve did? Would you even blame God to his face? 'The woman *you* put here with me ... It's your fault, God.' Would you do that? No, I suppose none of us would. Why, if God was there in front of us speaking to us, we wouldn't dare. We even feel a shiver of horror as we read Adam and Eve's brazen excuses.

Then why do we do it? Even though we do not see him, is he not there? Why do we pass the buck? When it comes to sin, why not begin to confess that the buck stops with us?

'So the LORD God said to the serpent, "Because you have done this, "Cursed are you above all the livestock and all the wild animals! You will crawl on your belly and you will eat dust all the days of your life. And I will put enmity between you and the woman, and between your offspring and hers; he will crush your head, and you will strike his heel"' (Genesis 3:14-15).

Here is the Lord Jesus Christ announcing what he himself will do![6] This first, great embryonic declaration of the gospel strikes hope in the souls of Adam and Eve and fear in the heart of the serpent. Do you not think it would massively encourage you to hear the Lord's condemnation and judgement of Satan? Would you not dance for joy if you heard the Lord Jesus Christ tell the devil of his own, ultimate victory over him?

But is it not just as true, even though you have not seen it with your own eyes or heard it with your own ears? It is believing the truth that sets us free, not seeing or hearing it. 'Blessed are those who have not seen and yet have believed' (John 20:29). Theophanies are wonderful because they help us picture what we want to see. However, then we have to recognise, 'We live by faith, not by sight' (2 Corinthians 5:7), and faith knows it is, in the end, the only secure way of grasping the truth.

How gracious of the Lord to announce the gospel before detailing the inevitable consequences of sin: 'To the woman he said, "I will greatly increase your pains in childbearing; with pain you will give birth to children. Your desire will be for your husband, and he will rule over you." To Adam he said, "Because you listened to your wife and ate from the tree about which I commanded you, 'You must not eat of it,' Cursed is the ground because of you; through painful toil you will eat of it all the days of your life. It will produce thorns and thistles for you, and you will eat the plants of the field. By the sweat of your brow you will eat your food until you return to the ground, since from it you were taken; for dust you are and to dust you will return"' (Genesis 3:16-19).

The Son of God lays out the essential elements of the curse, culminating in sin's ultimate penalty — death. Centuries later, the writer to the Hebrews was to insist, 'No discipline seems pleasant at the time, but painful. Later on, however, it produces a harvest of righteousness and peace for those who have been trained by it' (12:11). No doubt this was Adam and Eve's experience. They could never forget those dreadful words as they fell from the lips of the One with whom they had had such sweet communion. They could always picture the scene and, every time they remembered it, it seemed as though their hearts would break.

If only we could have such a vivid recall of the times the Lord has had to chasten us! Surely they would then need to be far less frequent. Do we not remember occasions when we had to hang our heads in shame as the Lord in great sorrow and disappointment lovingly had to chastise us for wilful sin? It is profitable to recall such times. Unlike Adam and Eve, or Peter in the high priest's courtyard (Luke 22:61), we have not seen the expression on our Saviour's face when we grieve him. Could we bear it if we did? What effect should it have upon us?

A shocking illustration

We must end this chapter with the glorious climax of the theophany in Eden, recorded in verse 21: 'The LORD God made garments of skin for Adam and his wife and clothed them.' Picture the scene. Here, in shocked silence and yet overwhelming gratitude, these two sinners learn that 'atonement', the usual translation in the Old Testament of the Hebrew word for 'covering', can only be provided by God himself through the shedding of blood. The Lord Jesus Christ makes the sacrifice from which the skins are obtained. By his own hand, death, 'the wages of sin' (Romans 6:23), enters the world. He removes the fig leaves they provided for themselves and covers their 'shameful nakedness' (Revelation 3:18).

In all this they were, they *had to be,* completely passive. What an illustration of the doctrine of justification by grace! Christ removes what Isaiah calls the 'filthy rags' of our own 'righteous acts' (64:6). What does the prophet say? 'I delight greatly in the LORD; my soul rejoices in my God. For he has clothed me with garments of salvation and arrayed me in a robe of righteousness' (61:10). He has done it; no one else! God's great plan of salvation is previewed in the Garden of Eden and the Son of God is already our great high priest.

Adam and Eve had still, of course, to be driven out of the Garden — they were sinners. But thank God they were saved sinners, eventually to gain, along with all true believers, far more than they had ever lost.

Notes

1 See, for example, Genesis 32:30; Judges 13:22.

2 **Walter Chalmers Smith**

3 **Josiah Conder**

4 The Puritan commentator **John Trapp,** much loved by C H Spurgeon, uses this expression in his notes on Genesis 1:27-28.

5 Luke 19:41; John 11:35; Hebrews 5:7.

6 That the Son of God here refers to himself in the third person is no significant objection to this interpretation. In the Gospels, Christ frequently refers to himself as the Son of Man—a title strikingly parallel to the woman's offspring.

Chapter 3

What faith must live with and without

Genesis 12:1-9

It may well have been normal for the Son of God to walk with Adam and Eve 'in the Garden in the cool of the day' (Genesis 3:8) but, once they had been banished because of sin, it was an altogether different story. Though the Lord continued to speak to them, he now did so clothed in clouds and thick darkness (Psalm 97:2). He is prepared to speak to Cain, but we do not read that he revealed himself. There was no theophany in those years following Eden. The centuries passed. Enoch and then Noah walked with God (Genesis 5:22, 6:9), but we no longer hear that God walked with them.

Two grievous judgments fell on a humanity devoted to going its own way. First, there came the Flood, but even that could not purge sin from the earth. It was still locked in the hearts of Noah and his family as they floated above the waters in the ark.

So the Lord decided to strike a second universal blow. Descending at the Tower of Babel he confused the languages of the people, routed their confederacy of evil and scattered them over the face of the planet. The scene was set for the Lord's next dramatic intervention in his great and glorious plan of salvation. The establishment of separate nations paved the way for the selection of the *one* nation, that was to be for two thousand years the exclusive repository and channel of God's revelation and redemption.

Therefore, we should not be surprised that at this crucial turning point in salvation history the Lord chooses to reveal himself to a human being, probably for the first time since the Garden of Eden became off limits. It is as though the Son of God cannot resist appearing, in order to reaffirm his gracious purposes and to indicate the new direction that those plans were about to take.

Ur of the Chaldeans

In order to continue the story, we need to leap forward a couple of millennia to events in the Book of Acts, not so radical a change of gear as it might seem. As the long seventh chapter opens, Stephen stands before the Jewish Sanhedrin council, accused of the terrible crimes of blasphemy and treason. 'Then the high priest asked him, "Are these charges true?" To this he replied: "Brothers and fathers, listen to me! The God of glory appeared to our father Abraham while he was still in Mesopotamia, before he lived in Haran"' (verses 1-2).

Now we know from Genesis 15:7 that the Lord brought Abraham out from 'Ur of the Chaldeans', but we have to wait over two thousand years before the Holy Spirit discloses that that first calling was by means of a theophany![1] 'The God of glory *appeared* to our father Abraham while he was still in Mesopotamia, before he lived in Haran.' That is something we are not told anywhere in the Old Testament. Notice also the title that Stephen here gives the Lord as he speaks of this theophany: 'the God of glory'. The apostle Paul, speaking of his longing for his own people Israel to be saved, declares, 'Theirs is the divine glory' (Romans 9:4) How appropriate that such a vision should be granted to Abraham, the father of the nation of Israel, at the very moment of his call!

You might find it worthwhile consulting the relevant map in the back of your Bible, to remind yourself where Abraham was when the Son of God appeared to him. You will find Ur just south of the River Euphrates, about 100 miles from the Persian Gulf. Also, if you are able to do so, make a point of visiting the British Museum. Among the vast treasures to be seen there, bringing to life virtually every period of biblical history, are some exquisite artefacts from Abraham's home town. From 1922 to 1934, Sir Leonard Woolley and his team excavated much of the ancient site. Ur is revealed to have been a prosperous trading port, its inhabitants highly cultured and sophisticated. The royal tombs, however, hid many dark secrets. For centuries, prior to and during the time of Abraham, the citizens of Ur had been in the grip of an idolatrous, cruel and bestial religion, routinely served by large-scale human sacrifice.

There is no suggestion anywhere in the Bible that Abraham was anything but thoroughly immersed in that thriving, but morally corrupt and spiritually bankrupt society. Indeed, the Scripture rather confirms this to be the case. Consider these words from the prophet Isaiah. 'Listen to me, you who pursue righteousness and who seek the LORD: Look to the rock from which you were cut and to the quarry from which you were hewn; look to Abraham, your father, and to Sarah, who gave you birth. When I called him he was but one, and I blessed him and made him many' (51:1-2).

In this interesting passage, Isaiah is trying to encourage a depressed people by reminding them how far the Lord has already brought them and how far he has yet to take them. This familiar formula is often prescribed for such cases in God's Word, but consider what is implied here regarding Abraham's origins. Who was Abraham? He was just like a shapeless lump of rock hewn from a dirty, dark and dismal quarry. That is what he was, spiritually speaking, when the God of glory first appeared to him in Ur of the Chaldeans.

Why, of all the people alive on the earth at the time, did God choose him? We always think of Abraham as being a great and godly man. That is what he certainly became, but it was not always so. And if God was nonetheless determined to choose him, why *just* him, why not others alongside him to give the new nation a better start? Things would have been much simpler if the Lord had also chosen his father and brothers.

But no, Isaiah says, 'When I called him he was but one.' One man alone is chosen. One man is to be the focus of God's purposes and the recipient of his saving grace. Then, just to render the Lord's plan even more baffling, we might care to bear in mind that the one chosen to be the father of a nation was already married to a woman who was unable to have children. You could say the Lord God enjoys a challenge. Or if you wanted to put it more theologically, you could say that the Lord loves to demonstrate his sovereign grace by selecting the hardest of cases. In this way, he also clearly derives most glory for himself.

Destination unknown

'The God of glory appeared to our father Abraham while he was still in

Mesopotamia, before he lived in Haran. 'Leave your country and your people,' God said, 'and go to the land I will show you' (Acts 7:2-3). This glorious appearance of the Son of God changed Abraham's life as radically and as immediately as did the theophany granted to Saul of Tarsus on the Damascus road. A theophany changes lives. We are going to see that time and time again as the history of the Old Testament patriarchs unfolds. Of course, this is hardly surprising; to put it mildly, a theophany is a crisis experience!

Abraham underwent a most dramatic conversion. Suddenly he was transformed from being a person who was fully immersed in the scene and culture of that idolatrous city of Ur to a servant of the Lord. His life was never to be the same from that moment on. He had never even heard of the true God until that time. Why should he have done? No one sought him in Ur. The people there had been immersed in idolatry and pagan worship for centuries. From birth, Abraham had known nothing else. Then, out of the blue, the Son of God appears to him and immediately he learns what he has to do. 'Leave your country and your people and go to the land I will show you.'

The command was as abrupt as it was startling, but he obeyed it. How on earth Abraham managed to persuade his father Terah and all their family and retinue to uproot and to leave a place where they were so comfortably off, I cannot imagine. 'But where do you want us to *go*, Abraham? You keep on telling us we have got to *go* somewhere. You say you have had this vision, or whatever, of "the one true God", as you call him. Now you say we have to leave our home for an unknown destination and you cannot even tell us why!' To which Abraham presumably replied, 'You're right, I'm sorry. I can tell you nothing else. All I know is we have to go and to do so as soon as possible.'

And so they went. Whether there was fierce and protracted argument we have no means of knowing, but Abraham prevailed. The lack of specific instruction was not as significant at the start as we might imagine. They went in the only obvious direction they really could, which was north-west up the Euphrates valley, following round what is known as the Fertile Crescent. Unless they had put out to sea, it is very difficult to imagine any other alternative, and they continued without settling anywhere until they came to a place called Haran, a distance of 600 miles.

It appears that it was there that Terah suddenly put his foot down, and said, 'Look, Abraham, enough is enough! This is a nice place, this Haran, and I'm staying here. You still seem to have no idea where you're going. Well, I am the head of the family. You do what you want, but the rest of us will not be going further.' Unwilling to cross his father at this point, and perhaps convincing himself that this was divine guidance, Abraham acquiesced. So the whole family settled down in Haran.

The gospel in advance

Then, one day, the Lord speaks to Abraham a second time and renews the call. Now is the time to turn to Genesis 12, with the realisation that this is not the account of Abraham's original call in Ur. Verse 1 reads, 'The LORD said to Abram . . .' If you are following in your Bible, forget the '*had* said'. The NIV follows the Authorised Version here without sufficient reason. The AV translators wanted to harmonise this passage with Abraham's first call as recorded in Acts 7. By using the possible, but unnatural, translation 'The LORD *had* said to Abram' in verse 1, they mean the reader to think back to the events in Ur. This is not only unnecessary, it is positively unhelpful. Most modern translations, for example the New American Standard Version, adopt the simpler and more accurate rendering.

'The LORD *said* to Abram, "Leave your country, your people, *and your father's household*, and go to the land I will show you."' The wording is very similar to that of the first call but with this very crucial addition in Haran. Now he is to leave his father and his father's family behind.[2]

My dilemma at this point is that this second call at Haran did not involve a theophany. Abraham heard God's voice, but we are not told that he saw God's form. Nevertheless, this call is so vital to an understanding of the story, quite apart from its immense theological and spiritual significance, that it would be impossible to ignore it. Abraham's great pilgrimage around the Fertile Crescent began and, as we shall see, ended with a theophany. Here in mid-journey, his call is renewed and refined, but along with it he receives a staggering sevenfold promise in Genesis 12:2-3.

'I will make you into a great nation.' That is the first promise. 'And I will bless you.' That is the second promise, assuring Abraham of *personal* prosperity. 'I will make your name great.' His name would be spoken about forever. And it is. We are speaking of it now. That is the third promise. 'And you will be a blessing.' It actually says, 'Be a blessing'. Abraham is to be a blessing to all those with whom he comes into contact. That is the fourth promise. 'I will bless those who bless you.' That is the fifth promise. 'And whoever curses you I will curse.' That is the sixth promise. These last two promises were demonstrated down the ages in the differing fates of Israel's friends and enemies. In varying degrees, all these promises were fulfilled in both Abraham the individual and the nation which sprang from him.

However, it is the seventh element of the seven-fold blessing that provides the greatest promise of all. 'And all peoples on earth will be blessed through you.' This is the second great gospel verse of the Bible. The first we considered in the previous chapter. There, in Genesis 3:15, the Lord promised to Adam and Eve that a Redeemer would be born who was fully human, 'the seed of the woman'. Here in Genesis 12, we have a narrowing of the focus. The promised Redeemer can no longer be potentially any member of the human race. We are now told the *nation* through whom the Redeemer will come. 'And all peoples on earth will be blessed through you.'

How can we be so certain that this is a full-blown Messianic prophecy? We have the assurance of the apostle Paul, who declares in Galatians 3:8, 'The Scripture foresaw that God would justify the Gentiles by faith and *announced the gospel in advance* to Abraham: "All nations will be blessed through you."'

Into the Promised Land

So Abraham obeys the call and leaves Haran, this time without his father and probably the bulk of his father's household and retinue. He still has no idea where he is going, but he continues on in the logical direction around Fertile Crescent of well-watered land that had already been populated and cultivated by various peoples for generations. Crossing the upper reaches of the great River Euphrates, he continues westwards to Aleppo. Turning south to follow the Orontes river valley, he passes through Lebanon and eventually enters the land of Canaan itself. Remember, he still has no inkling that he has reached his destination. Nor does the Lord give him any such indication until he reaches the very heart of Canaan at a place called Shechem. Once there, however, not only does God once more break his silence but he appears to him again as he had those many years before at Ur. Abraham was about to experience his second theophany.

'Abram travelled through the land as far as the site of the great tree of Moreh at Shechem. At that time the Canaanites were in the land. The Lord appeared to Abram and said, "To your offspring I will give this land." So he built an altar there to the LORD, who had appeared to him' (Genesis 12:6-7).

Though it signals the end of the patriarch's quest, this is by no means the last of the preincarnate Son of God's appearances to Abraham. No wonder the Lord Jesus Christ told the Jews, 'Your father Abraham rejoiced to see my day, and he saw it and was glad' (John 8:56).

What a thrill it must have been for Abraham to see the Lord as he had decades earlier back in Ur of the Chaldeans! In this second theophany, the Lord Jesus Christ announces the fulfilment of the promise that he made in the first. 'To your offspring I will give this land.' In other words, 'This is it, Abraham. You have arrived at last.' After a pilgrimage of over a thousand miles, the land that Abraham seems to have reached purely by chance proves to be the place of God's choosing after all.

'From there he went on toward the hills east of Bethel and pitched his tent, with Bethel on the west and Ai on the east. There he built an altar to the LORD and called on the name of the LORD. Then Abram set out and continued towards the Negev' (Genesis 12:8-9). What is he doing? He wants to traverse the whole of the land that his descendants were to possess. He wants to see it for himself! Wouldn't you?

You may well have been making spiritual applications for yourself as we have rushed through the history of Abraham's call. I did not want to interrupt the flow of the account and I wanted you to notice the wonderful symmetry in God's dealings with Abraham from the first theophany at the beginning of the call to the second theophany at its fulfilment. But now it might be helpful to have some of the practical lessons spelt out a little more explicitly. Let me draw out a number that seem to lie very close to the surface.

The key factor in the life of Abraham was his faith. This is epitomised in that wonderful statement seized on by the apostle Paul to demonstrate God's means of justifying the sinner. 'Abraham believed the Lord, and he credited it to him as righteousness' (Genesis 15:6). Abraham believed God, and his trust in God's Word and God's promise of a Messiah brought him salvation.

The fact that this was no mere intellectual belief is revealed by its outworking in practical obedience. More is rightly made of Abraham's faith in that great chapter on the subject, Hebrews 11, than of anybody else's. Granted that the great individual acts of Abraham's faith, like for example his preparedness to sacrifice his son Isaac, still lay in the future, the account of the pilgrimage from Ur to Canaan is alone sufficient for us to isolate some of the basic characteristics of a life of true faith.

For the sake of simplicity, let us say that there are some things that faith must live with, and other things that faith must live without.

What faith must live with

Faith must live with uncertainty. I know there are many Christians who hate that fact, and I don't blame them. Most of us prefer certainty. Those who like to live on the edge and enjoy the excitement of never knowing what is going to happen next tend to be somewhat rare. Moreover, their rarity increases with age! But the fact of the matter is that the life of faith means that we have to live with uncertainty. In Hebrews 11 we read, 'By faith Abraham, when called to go to a place he would later receive as his inheritance, obeyed and went, even though he did not know where he was going' (verse 8). That was true all the way and all the time.

If Abraham had demanded to know the whole story before leaving Ur, he would never have left. He would have stayed in Ur until the day he died, for the simple reason that the Lord had decided he would be told at the end of the journey and not the beginning. Thankfully, Abraham was enabled to provide us with an awesome display of what it means to walk by faith and not by sight (2 Corinthians 5:7). His method was to proceed by taking reasonable steps in a logical direction as they presented themselves. In other words, he used sanctified common sense, which is surely nowhere better illustrated in the Bible than here. How else did he arrive in the Promised Land with no evidence of direct guidance? When God said, 'Move' and there was only one direction in which to go, no further miraculous intervention was required. So it was not surprising, at least to the eye of faith, that at the end of a long journey, Abraham found himself in exactly the right place.

There are wonderful rewards for those who are prepared to face up to the uncertainties of life and walk by faith. Christians who insist on walking by sight often find that they are standing still for long periods. If you insist on waiting until things are absolutely crystal clear and everything is spelt out to the last detail before you are prepared to move, you will never do anything. Of course, it only needs a few respected church members to think like that, for a congregation to lie moribund for years. Many churches make little progress because they want it all spelt out. Where is the operation of faith? Those who would walk by faith must live with a degree of uncertainty.

Faith must live with heartache and bewilderment. I put these together because they were certainly together in Abraham's experience. How did Abraham feel about his childlessness in a society that considered it to be a curse, especially in the light of the Lord's promise that all people on earth would be blessed through him? How did his wife, Sarah, feel?[3] It was a major factor in their marriage from the very beginning. Virtually the first thing we learn about either of them in the Scriptures is that Sarah was 'barren' (Genesis 11:30). It was something that seemed to hold them back and to hamper their service for God even after they had been called by him.

How often it seems that those who are potentially going to be the most useful to the kingdom of God are dogged by providential circumstances that prevent or at least hinder their ministry. We shake our heads and appear to wonder whether the Lord truly knows what he is doing. Maybe in your own life and experience you have certain regrets you look back on and say, 'I had my heart set on serving the Lord in this particular way, but he never made it possible.'

Have you never realised from your reading of the Bible that faith must live with heartache and bewilderment? Did you not understand that they are part of God's purposes for each of us in our lives? Through them faith is encouraged to trust more and more in the hand of a wise and a loving heavenly Father. It is part of the very essence of the outworking and strengthening of our faith that these things must occur.

Faith must live with trials and opposition. Bear in mind that the Promised Land was not exactly empty! When the Lord brought Abraham down there he did not say, 'Now look, Abraham, here is this marvellous place to live, a land flowing with milk and honey, and nobody has found it yet! It is completely empty and you can live in it happily ever after with all your descendants.' It was not like that. The place was full, positively crowded compared with many areas on the earth's surface. Moreover, those in residence were hostile and pagan tribes who had absolutely no intention of handing Canaan over to some strange foreigner who turned up claiming that God had told him it was his!

Just to compound matters, no sooner had Abraham entered the land but a famine forced him to leave it and go on down to Egypt.[4] Then the problems and trials really started to mount up. Again, we are tempted to ask whether the Lord has a coherent plan. But the fact is, it is all part of the journey of faith. Faith must live with trials and opposition.

The apostle Peter was writing to deeply distressed believers when he gave this assurance: 'all kinds of trials . . . come so that your faith — of greater worth than gold, which perishes even though refined by fire — may be proved genuine and may result in praise, glory and honour when Jesus Christ is revealed' (1 Peter 1:6 and 7). In fact, it is impossible to think or a great man or woman of faith who has not known trial and opposition. Without such difficulties, their faith would not have been revealed.

What Faith must live without

Let us close this chapter by considering two things that faith must live without. *Faith must sometimes live without what is dear to us.* In Abraham's case, this meant he had to live without his country, his people and (most significantly of all) his father's household. It is clear that that last item was always going to be the hardest. How faithful and merciful was Abraham's God, who would not let his servant be tempted beyond what he could bear.[5] The Lord knew the separation would ultimately be inevitable but he was prepared to wait until Abraham realised it for himself, until the second call came at Haran.

Abraham evidently loved his father very much. He must have pleaded very earnestly with Terah to come with him from Ur. Yet Terah never abandoned his idolatrous views. In the Book of Joshua we are told explicitly, 'Terah worshipped other gods' (24:2). Terah held Abraham back spiritually. Humanly speaking, Abraham might have been in the Promised Land years earlier had it not been for his father. Finally at Haran, Abraham is instructed to leave him. 'Leave your country, your people, *and your father's household* and go to the land I will show you' (Genesis 12:1).

A textual problem that has vexed commentators over the centuries may well cast a favourable sidelight on this interpretation. Stephen says in Acts 7:4 that Abraham did not leave Haran until after his father had died, whereas, in fact, if you do your arithmetic in Genesis, it is clear that Terah lived on in Haran for a further sixty years after Abraham had departed.[6] Every attempt at harmonising this apparent inconsistency is fraught with difficulties.

Perhaps we should be seeking a solution that is rather more spiritual than mathematical. Even today, those who defect from Judaism are considered by the orthodox adherent to be 'dead'. It is as though they no longer existed, a traditional view which stretches back over the centuries. Is this what Stephen had in mind? Perhaps the old opinion is right that suggests Abraham had to come to the point where he could accept that *spiritually* his father was dead. His father worshipped idols. He was not a convert to the one true God and the messianic promise. His presence in Canaan would have been incongruous. Even had he been willing to enter the land on his own terms, it would not have been permitted.

A potential disciple once came to the Lord Jesus and pleaded, 'Lord, first let me go and bury my father' (Matthew 8:21). It is probably best not to assume that in this instance the father had already died. After all, people were buried on the same day. If that were the case here, Jesus' famous answer would appear callous and unfeeling. No, much better to take it that the father was obviously elderly and the son thought he had better stay at home for the last few years of his father's life and then maybe he would follow Christ.

'But Jesus told him, "Follow me, and let the dead bury their own dead"' (Matthew 8:22). In other words, let the spiritually dead bury the spiritually dead, when eventually they also die physically. What has a Christian disciple got to do with the spiritually dead? In a similar way, Abraham's course of action was equally clear.

The application for us is plain. If we are involved in relationships which are hampering our Christian service or are holding us back from entering into the promises of God's Word, then we must radically disengage ourselves. We need to be able to vow, along with the Apostle Paul, 'May I never boast except in the cross of our Lord Jesus Christ, through which the world has been crucified to me, and I to the world' (Galatians 6:14).

One final thought is that *faith must sometimes live without receiving the promised blessing in its lifetime*. Abraham was one of several in the list of heroes of the faith in Hebrews 11 of whom it was said, 'They all did not receive the things promised; they only saw them and welcomed them from a distance' (verse 13). Stephen said of Abraham, 'God gave him no inheritance here, not even a foot of ground' (Acts 7:5). He was an alien and a stranger in the Promised Land. That is why it has been memorably remarked, 'Abraham pitched his tents but built his altars'. He left behind him not the signs of wealth but of worship. He gave up all that he had for divine promises from which he never personally benefitted on earth. Yet he would have said that he had given up so little and received so much.

But, Abraham, the Promised Land was never yours! 'True,' Abraham would reply, 'but it belonged to my descendants. The Lord God gave it to me for them. All right, I never possessed it. I could never call a foot of it my own but, in the end, God's promises to me were wonderfully fulfilled.'

There are many things dear to our hearts that we might make the object of believing prayer year after year. We may never live to see our prayers answered as we would wish, but our faith may well bear fruit beyond our lifetime on this earth. I think of Martyn Lloyd-Jones, who prayed all his life for true spiritual revival but never saw it. Nevertheless, his prayers will be answered, maybe in our day. Whatever happens, though genuine faith must often live without receiving the promise, it need not faint. For faith is not nourished by receiving blessing but by trusting God.

Notes

1 Though 'Abram' does not become 'Abraham' until Genesis 17:5, it is simpler to maintain the more familiar name throughout, except where quoting Scripture.

2 Attempts to refer the call of Genesis 12:1 back to Ur involve the added disadvantage of rendering Abraham disobedient. He did not leave his father's household until he left Haran.

3 'Sarah' is properly 'Sarai' until Genesis 17:15. See note 1.

4 Genesis 12:10.

5 See 1 Corinthians 10:13.

6 Compare Genesis 11:26, 11:32 and 12:4.

Two simple questions

Genesis 15

Shortly after the Lord appeared to Abraham in Shechem, confirming that he had indeed arrived in the Promised Land, the patriarch was to learn one of the most humiliating lessons of his life. Choosing to go down to Egypt to escape a famine, for reasons of personal safety he had decided to pass off his wife as his sister. As a result, he was rebuked for a lack of moral integrity and sent packing by a pagan Pharaoh[1]. Despite his having become 'very wealthy in livestock and in silver and gold' (Genesis 13:2) during this period, the spiritual cost had been enormous.

As a result of that shameful incident, he left Egypt, resolved to sit very light to the things of the world. Like his descendant Moses, from now on it could be said of Abraham, 'He chose to be ill-treated along with the people of God rather than to enjoy the pleasures of sin for a short time. He regarded disgrace for the sake of Christ as of greater value than the treasures of Egypt, because he was looking ahead to his reward' (Hebrews 11:25-26).

Abraham happily allowed his nephew Lot to choose the fertile pastures of the Jordan Plain when a quarrel broke out between their respective herdsmen and a separation was indicated[2]. The Lord was immediately pleased with this further distancing of himself from his father's household, especially as it was clearly costly. 'The Lord said to Abram after Lot had parted from him, "Lift up your eyes from where you are and look north and south, east and west. All the land that you see I will give to you and your offspring for ever. I will make your offspring like the dust of the earth, so that if anyone could count the dust, then your offspring could be counted. Go, walk through the length and breadth of the land, for I am giving it to you." So Abram moved his tents and went to live near the great trees of Mamre at Hebron, where he built an altar to the LORD' (Genesis 13:14-18).

Because he was content to give up the best of the land, the Lord announced he would give him all of it. 'Blessed are the meek, for they will inherit the earth' (Matthew 5:5). Our attitude to material possessions has a great bearing on the spiritual blessings we receive.

Melchizedek—king of Salem

For some years, apparently, Abraham lives and worships happily at Hebron in the south of Canaan. One further incident must be mentioned before we come to the next record of theophany, because it culminates in one of the most mysterious and tremendous encounters of the Old Testament[3]. One day, Abraham hears that Lot has been captured by foreign troops during a punitive raiding expedition on the cities of the plains. Then we learn something most extraordinary. Abraham manages to assemble a small military force from his household and becomes something of a warrior. No doubt with supernatural aid he manages to rescue not only Lot but also the people and goods that had been plundered from the local towns. When he returns, the king of Sodom, who is delighted to see the captives brought home, bids Abraham keep the booty for himself. At which point, the patriarch makes a very noble speech, once again indicating his attitude to material goods. 'But Abram said to the king of Sodom, "I have raised my hand to the LORD, God Most High, Creator of heaven and earth, and have taken an oath that I will accept nothing belonging to you, not even a thread or the thong of a sandal, so that you will never be able to say, 'I made Abraham rich'"' (Genesis 14:22-23).

This whole episode is most renowned, however, for the introduction onto the scene of the enigmatic Melchizedek, king of Salem. It is very tempting to regard Melchizedek as a theophany, but it is safer to think of him as perhaps the very last representative of the old order of true believers.

'Then Melchizedek king of Salem brought out bread and wine. He was priest of God Most High, and he blessed Abram, saying, "Blessed be Abram by God Most High, Creator of heaven and earth. And blessed be God Most High, who delivered your enemies into your hand." Then Abram gave him a tenth of everything' (Genesis 14:18-20). Melchizedek was a spiritual successor to Noah. Once again, the world had grown so evil that God determined to take extraordinary measures to preserve both the truth and the human line from which the Saviour would eventually appear. The answer this time was not to be a Flood but the creation of a specially privileged and protected nation.

We may helpfully interpret the scene before us as depicting the torch being handed on from the old dispensation to the new. No longer was a residue of true believers to be simply scattered throughout the peoples of the world. One people was to be chosen by God to act as the repository and guardian of his great plan of redemption until the day of its fulfilment. Melchizedek is here virtually transferring his title to the land to Abraham and his descendants. Both men recognise that they are recipients of the same grace, servants of the same God Most High. It is a little like the old prophet Simeon in the temple not willing to depart until he has held the infant Christ in his arms and greeted the new-born hope[4]. Yet, of course, Melchizedek is far more even than this. He is a perfect type of Christ, as Psalm 110 and the letter to the Hebrews reveal.

Seeing the Word

But enough! We are not dealing with types, but theophanies! So we enter the strange world of Genesis 15. 'After this, the Word of the Lord came to Abram in a vision' (verse 1). Now just think about that for a moment. How does the Word come in a vision? How can you see the Word of the Lord? Well, of course our subject alerts us to what is happening and various other aspects of the remarkable events recorded here confirm that this is the right and only plausible explanation. We know as Christian believers that 'the Word became flesh and made his dwelling among us.' The apostle John goes on to say, 'We have seen his glory' (John 1:14). The Word is one of our Saviour's most significant titles. The Lord Jesus Christ is the living Word, or as he describes himself in the last book of the Bible, 'the Alpha and the Omega,' (Revelation 1:8). What is meant by that? Jesus declares himself to be the first and last letters of the Greek alphabet, so encapsulating the sum of all that can be communicated by a holy God to sinful people.

This is in fact the first reference in the Bible to 'the Word of the Lord' and it is surely no coincidence that it involves a theophany. Here in Genesis 15 we are introduced not primarily to the spoken Word of God that is heard, but to the living Word of God who is seen. Furthermore, when he does speak, what he declares is the first of the glorious 'I am' texts of Scripture, which the New Testament causes us to associate so much with the Lord Jesus Christ himself (verse 1).

'After this, the Word of the Lord came to Abram in a vision: "Do not be afraid, Abram, I am your shield, your very great reward.' This theophany itself is a gracious reward for the faith, love, courage and generosity that Abraham has been displaying. He has evidently learnt great lessons from his humiliation in Egypt, and the Lord comes to him to encourage him. Though, to all outward appearance, Abraham seemed strong, confident and perfectly in control of the situation, appearances can be deceptive.

The Lord knew that inwardly his servant was fearful. Perhaps he was afraid of the human enemies he had made. After all, by some amazing divine intervention and with just a handful of men he had turned the tables on a strong and ruthless invading force. Those kings were not likely to forget their embarrassing defeat. Probably, they would be back. He might understandably have thought, 'I'm not going to get away with that again.' He may have had natural fears along those lines. More fundamental, however, as we shall see, were the underlying spiritual concerns that threatened to engulf him. The Lord knew he had good reason to say to his servant, 'Do not be afraid'.

At a natural level, the Son of God assures Abraham that he need fear no pagan marauders: 'I am your shield'. Nor should Abraham ever permit the evil one to make him wish he had accepted the riches of Sodom that had been pressed upon him: 'I am your very great reward'. When will the children of Abraham learn the lesson he learnt and exercise their father's faith? How many believers have never truly experienced the Lord as their 'shield' because they have never taken risks of faith on his behalf? And how many have never known the Lord as their reward because they prefer the trinkets of the world?

So often we hold on desperately to the things of the world and so miss out horribly on the spiritual blessings of God. To live in sole dependence on the Lord as our 'shield' and in sole expectation of the Lord as our 'reward' would lead us directly to the heart of God and into intense communion with him. That is the experience of true men and women of God in every age. Is it ours?

How to complain

You may have read through this fifteenth chapter of Genesis many times and never really come to understand the strange ritual which forms its centrepiece. Certainly, what occurs here, particularly in the latter part of the chapter, seems to be extremely mysterious and utterly alien to anything with which we are familiar. Nonetheless, what takes place is actually in response to two very simple questions put by Abraham — two very simple questions that you and I have probably asked repeatedly throughout our Christian lives.

The two questions are these: 'What can you give me?' in verse 2 and 'How can I know?' in verse 8. Sadly, many Christians seem to go through the whole of their lives never receiving answers to these fundamental questions. No wonder they are always plagued with doubts, never producing the spiritual fruit that might have been expected.

'What can you give me?' The universal meaning of the first question is this: 'What on earth, Lord, can you do in the circumstances in which I find myself?' Believers seem to lurch from one crisis to another, in which they do not see how the Lord can possibly work. The second question 'How can I know?' is equally basic. 'How can I be sure that the Lord will deliver the promises that I believe he has made to me?' That is a very real question for the many Christians who are spiritually paralysed through the fear of uncertainty.

As we look at these questions in their context, we need to keep verse 1 in our minds. Only those whose dependence is on God as their 'shield' and whose expectation is in God as their 'reward' will ask these basic questions in a way that will receive an answer. If we truly want a reply, we must come in the same reverent submission and faith as Abraham here.

Incidentally, both of the questions asked of Christ in this extended theophany, which lasted, as we shall see, anything up to 24 hours, are prefaced with the words, 'But Abram said. . .' The Lord makes two glorious declarations in verses 1 and 7; in fact, they are staggering personal promises to Abraham. Yet, in both instances the man comes straight back with an objection, 'But Abram said. . .' Is this bordering on blasphemous ingratitude? No, it is a consequence of the intimacy and confidence of faith, as the Lord's responses confirm. Those who never complain *about* God will be heard when they complain *to* him.

Many Christians complain *about* God. They say, 'Why has the Lord done this?' They mutter to one another. They do not think it is fair—this should not happen, that should not happen. They complain about the Lord's work and the Lord's people, failing to understand that those who really want to get answers to fundamental questions should stop complaining *about* God and start complaining *to* him.

Of course, a lot of people do both. That is no good either. God ignores those who complain *to* him as long as they are still complaining *about* him. Those who never complain *about* God will be heard when they complain *to* him. That is the great secret of the success in prayer enjoyed not only by Abraham, but by Moses, David, Elijah and a whole host of other giants of the faith, both within and beyond the pages of the Bible.

The greatest saints do not have fewer heartaches, puzzles and dilemmas in their lives than anybody else. They only *seem* to because they refuse to complain about them to their fellow creatures, preferring to take them to the Lord for him to sort out.

What can you give me?

'But Abram said, "O Sovereign LORD, *what can you give me* since I remain childless and the one who will inherit my estate is Eliezer of Damascus?" And Abram said, "You've given me no children; so a servant in my household will be my heir" (Genesis 15:2-3). Suddenly, it all comes out in a rush. For the first time, God's servant reveals the real root of his ongoing fears and doubts. Listen, as he complains to the Lord. 'You keep on saying you are going to make me a great nation. How can you be my reward when this reward you keep on telling me about is going to come through my children? I have no children, nor am I likely to have any. And that is your doing. You have not given my wife the ability to bear children. So what are you saying, Lord? Have I got it all wrong? When you spoke of my "offspring" in Shechem, was I taking it all too literally? Do you really mean to fulfil your promises to me through my legal heir, Eliezer of Damascus?'

To all of this, the Son of God gives a patient and gracious dual response. First, 'The word of the LORD came to him: "This man will not be your heir, but a son coming from your own body will be your heir"' (Genesis 15:4). That is the first time Abraham has heard that spelt out unambiguously. The Lord here shares a little more of the detail of his plan. The promise is being made more explicit. Now there can be no mistake; he has heard it, literally, from the Lord's own lips!

Having extended his understanding, the Son of God now takes Abraham by the hand for a simple reminder of his power. 'He took him outside and said, "Look up at the heavens and count the stars — if indeed you can count them." Then he said to him, "So shall your offspring be"' (Genesis 15:5). Nothing could have been more simple or more effective, providing the setting, as it does, for one of the most significant verses in the Bible. 'Abram believed the LORD, and he credited it to him as righteousness' (Genesis 15:6). This is not of course to be thought of as the moment of Abraham's conversion. That had happened years previously back in Ur. This is, nevertheless, a breakthrough development in his faith and is particularly poignant when seen in the context of this theophany. Not only is the subject of the Messianic line under discussion, the Messiah himself has been leading the conversation. Additionally, when it says here that Abraham 'believed the Lord', it is the Lord Jesus Christ himself, in theophany, that he is trusting! The use of this text in the New Testament to demonstrate that salvation can only be, and has always been, a product of justification by faith in Christ, appears more wonderfully appropriate than ever.

Returning to the immediate circumstances in our passage, Abraham's fears about God's ability to bless him as he promised have been removed very simply. All the Lord needed to do was to reveal a little more of his plan and give a simple reminder of his power and the 'impossible' situation was resolved.

The Lord works similarly for us, when humbly we seek solutions to apparently impossible circumstances. Maybe you find yourself absolutely trapped in a cul-de-sac, and you cannot remotely see any way out. You cannot see that there is anything that God can do. God himself seems to have painted himself into a corner. That is precisely what Abraham thought in verse 2. Perhaps the Lord will make the same gracious, dual response to you. He will often reveal to our understanding a little more of his plan and purpose for us. Through studying the Word of God we may frequently discover fresh insights or details that help us understand a little more of the way the Lord is working things out in our lives.

Then again, as with Abraham, our God may well grant us a new experience of his glorious power and omnipotence. It may well come through gazing at the sky on a clear night. Even despite the dust and light pollution of modern urban society, the knowledge that the same 'hands that flung stars into space'[5] have a secure hold on you may well put your doubts and fears into perspective.

Sometimes, it may be that there is an experience at the opposite end of the spectrum. I remember reading about Mungo Park, the pioneer explorer of West Africa at the end of the 18th and beginning of the 19th centuries. Apparently once he became very frightened because he was utterly lost and could see no way out of the situation. Just as he was about to succumb to a feeling of hopelessness and abject self pity he suddenly stooped down and marvelled at the intricate beauty of a small patch of moss at his feet. As he studied it and noted the amazing patterns and detail of this small plant that probably no one else had ever seen, or would ever see, he thought to himself, 'God is at work even here; why should I be afraid?'

As the Lord expands our understanding and experience of his working, we discover that we can walk by faith where once we thought we would only be able to walk by sight. Understanding and experience should grow together. A mature grasp of basic scriptural principles married to a broad experience of God's working in his children's lives will often cast light on the gloomiest of circumstances. Even where nothing has essentially changed, we may find that we are now able to look on things altogether differently.

How can I know?

We come now to the second of Abraham's two simple questions asked in the course of this theophany. Once again, God speaks: '"I am the LORD, who brought you out of Ur of the Chaldeans to give you this land to take possession of it." But Abram said, "O Sovereign Lord, *how can I know* that I will gain possession of it?"' (Genesis 15:7-8). Here is Abraham's second complaint to God. It is as though he says, 'I now realise that you *can* bring your promises to pass but could I not have greater assurance that you *will*? How can I know?'

Little did Abraham imagine that this humble complaint would draw forth such an extraordinary response from God, a response that was to lead to a far from pleasant experience for Abraham. Requests for assurance in relation to supposed divine promises or guidance are frequently met in ways that we would not choose.

'But Abram said, "O Sovereign LORD, how can I know that I shall gain possession of it?" So the LORD said to him, "Bring me a heifer, a goat and a ram, each three years old, along with a dove and a young pigeon,"' (Genesis 15:8-9). All of the five animals that were later to be allowed for sacrificial purposes under the law of Moses are named here. The next verse continues, 'Abram brought all these to him, cut them in two and arranged the halves opposite each other; the birds, however, he did not cut in half,' presumably placing one on either side (Genesis 15:10). So the pieces of these animals are put in two rows, with a corridor between them. Even though he was not told, Abraham knew what to do. It was evident to him that the Lord wished to establish a covenant. A literal translation of verse 18 would read, 'On that day the LORD *cut* a covenant with Abram'.

The procedure was known and well-established in those days. The custom required the severing of animals in halves; then the two parties to this solemn, binding agreement, this covenant, would pass between the butchered pieces. The implication was that if either were to break the covenant, then their life would be forfeit, as the lives of the animals had been.

Abraham arranges the ritual. By now the stars have paled in the sky and morning has broken. At some stage, the Lord disappears from the scene. Abraham is alone. He waits and waits. 'Then birds of prey came down on the carcasses, but Abram drove them away' (Genesis 15:11). There is a wonderful verse for spiritualising! You can make the 'birds of prey' stand for anything that might swoop down and seek to spoil your worship or Christian service. However, there is more than enough in this passage without having to read things into it.

The hours pass as Abraham guards the ritual scene. Remember, Abraham has been awake most of the previous night, when he had been taken out by God to consider the stars in the sky. It is no wonder that we read in verse 12, 'As the sun was setting, Abram fell into a deep sleep, and a thick and dreadful darkness came over him.' I am sure there are many here who know something of what it is to be suddenly overwhelmed with this 'thick and dreadful darkness'. Do not let Satan persuade you that there is nobody in Scripture or in history itself who could comprehend what you are going through. 'No temptation has seized you except what is common to man' (1 Corinthians 10:13). It is pride that causes us to imagine we are enduring an experience unique in its severity. 'Nobody else could understand the fears, the doubts, the misery I am feeling. . .' That is simply untrue.

Spiritually speaking, that 'thick and dreadful darkness' may take many forms. Maybe even as you are reading these lines, you yourself are feeling totally besieged by appalling doubts and temptations, overwhelmed by a sense of utter loneliness, futility or uselessness, Perhaps you are the victim of the crushing juggernaut of a weary and desperate depression.

I want you to notice that this was part of God's answer to Abraham's question, 'How can I know?' Those who would know the greatest joys in the life of faith must generally experience the greatest sorrows. Why? Because the Lord would have us understand something of what it cost him to deliver us from the misery of sin. He wants to see no glib, careless, presumptuous assurance in his children. There is plenty of that around today and it gives neither true glory to God, nor true peace to the believer.

Is Abraham exposed here to an apprehension of some of the dreadful suffering of his descendants? 'As the sun was setting, Abram fell into a deep sleep, and a thick and dreadful darkness came over him. Then the LORD said to him, "Know for certain that your descendants will be strangers in a country not their own, and they will be enslaved and ill-treated four hundred years. But I will punish the nation they serve as slaves, and afterward they will come out with great possessions. You, however, will go to your fathers in peace and be buried at a good old age. In the fourth generation your descendants will come back here, for the sin of the Amorites has not yet reached its full measure"' (Genesis 15:12-16).

What secrets are revealed to him here! God draws aside the veil of the future and reveals to him the captivity of Israel, their eventual release from Egypt and their ultimate possession of Canaan! We, of course, who have read Genesis and Exodus know even the details. What is more, we know that Israel's slavery and ultimate deliverance into the Promised Land are but a picture of the dreadful bondage of sin and the wonderful redemption that has been won for us by the Lord Jesus Christ upon the cross.

Those who know the greatest assurance of salvation have felt the dreadful darkness of sin dispelled by the light of Christ. Why did the Lord make Abraham wait by the carcasses throughout the long hours of that day? He was made to wait until it seemed to him that death and darkness were winning the vigil. God knew he needed to learn patience. It would still be some years before Isaac was born. It would still be some centuries before Israel would possess the Promised Land. It would still be millennia before the Lord Jesus Christ would come and all the nations be blessed. Is the Lord teaching you to wait patiently?

At last, he comes. 'When the sun had set and darkness had fallen, a smoking brazier with a blazing torch appeared and passed between the pieces' (Genesis 15:17). Notice that only the Lord, now taking upon himself this obscure fiery form, passes between the butchered animals. It is a strange, one-sided covenant; but then the covenants of God always are. At the end of it all, Abraham seems to have no part to play, no obligation to fulfil. It is a covenant all of grace. 'On that day the LORD made a covenant with Abram and said, "To your descendants I give this land, from the river of Egypt to the great river, the Euphrates

— the land of the Kenites, Kenizzites, Kadmonites, Hittites, Perizzites, Rephaites, Amorites, Canaanites, Girgashites and Jebusites"' (Genesis 15:18-21).

'Praise to the Lord, who, when darkness and sin are abounding,
Who, when the godless to triumph, all virtue confounding,
Sheddeth his light,
Chaseth the horrors of night,
Saints with his mercy surrounding.'[6]

You may know 'the horrors of night' but you may also know the joys of the light through the Lord Jesus Christ. He is the covenant-keeping God who knows and understands all things and whose promises never fail. He is patient with us. We can afford to be patient with him.

This covenant was cut and sealed in the blood of animals. There can be no covenant without forgiveness. There can be no forgiveness without the shedding of blood. Thank God for the One who came and said, "This cup is the new covenant in my blood, which is poured out for you' (Luke 22:20).

Notes

1. Genesis 12:10-20
2. Genesis 13:5-12
3. Genesis 14
4. Luke 2:25-35
5. **Graham Kendrick**, *The Servant King*.
6. Joachim Neander, 'Praise to the Lord, the Almighty, the King of creation' (translated by **Catherine Winkworth**).

The God who sees me

Genesis 16

We have struck a vein of Scripture rich in theophany and shall find ourselves examining several consecutive chapters of the Book of Genesis. Yet this is hardly surprising, because these chapters describe the foundation of the nation from which the Son of God would be born as the Son of Man. No wonder he is so keen to be with his people at this embryonic stage of their development. Theophanies recur, and we marvel to see the Saviour managing and overseeing the beginnings of the process that would ultimately result in his incarnation.

We have seen how, in answer to Abraham's growing fears about the fulfilment of the promise, the Lord assures him, a son '*coming from your own body*' would be his heir (Genesis 15:4). That very specific and unambiguous pledge gave him great comfort, despite his wife Sarah's inability to conceive and his own advancing years.

Sarah — an example to follow

By the time we enter Chapter 16, however, a few more years have actually passed and a weary and puzzled Sarah decides to take matters into her own hands. 'Now Sarai, Abram's wife, had borne him no children. But she had an Egyptian maidservant named Hagar; so she said to Abram, "The LORD has kept me from having children. Go, sleep with my maidservant; perhaps I can build a family through her." Abram agreed to what Sarai said. So after Abram had been living in Canaan ten years, Sarai his wife took her Egyptian maidservant Hagar and gave her to her husband to be his wife. He slept with Hagar, and she conceived' (Genesis 16:1-4).

Remembering that the apostle Peter holds up Sarah as the mother of all godly wives,[1] we would be very wise not to jump too quickly to a sweeping condemnation of her lack of faith. Her motive, without any doubt whatsoever, is absolutely pure and unimpeachable. She desperately wants God's promise to be fulfilled and, as any godly person should when a clear promise of God is being delayed, she looks to herself. She is a shining example in this respect.

We shall come to her failings soon enough, we can afford to dwell on this aspect for a moment. She asks herself the question, 'Am I the impediment here?' She thinks back on what has been said. Abraham has been told that a son shall come from his own body, but there was no specific mention that this son would come from *hers*. Maybe she is just too sinful for God to use. Maybe God intends to bypass her in his plan and the delay is simply until she comes to realise this for herself. Of course! How gentle God has been to her! How patiently her poor husband has suffered! How wicked and blind and selfish she has been! These are the kind of thoughts, I am persuaded, were going through the mind of this godly, but sadly mistaken woman.

At this juncture, she is wholly humble and submissive. There is none of Rachel's angry 'Give me children, or I'll die!' (Genesis 30:1). No, she accepts it with holy resignation. It is without any resentment that she declares, 'The LORD has kept me from having children' (verse 2).

Moreover, her offer to Abraham of a surrogate wife and mother, which seems so completely immoral and bizarre to us, was then both a common, legally and culturally acceptable solution to such a difficulty. Selflessly, despite the ongoing pain and humiliation she would inevitably suffer, she was prepared to take the initiative in suggesting the plan.

We might even add in her defence that here at least was a woman who was prepared to seek to cooperate with the Lord. Many of us are perfectly content to sit back and expect the Lord God to do everything. Does the Lord not expect us to use our common sense and initiative in helping to bring his purposes to pass? Is it not true that 'God helps those who help themselves'? Well, not in this case, though it might well help some rather passive believers to consider the possibility in their own!

Doctrinal and spiritual failure

In spite of all of these mitigating circumstances, Abraham and Sarah failed here, in both doctrinal understanding and in practical spirituality.

Doctrinally, they fell down in that both of them would have been aware that God created one woman for Adam. However the Word of God had been passed down to them, they would have known that the divine pattern laid down from the creation was that only two can become one flesh. Their failure to acknowledge this and instead to conform to the standards of the world round about them in this regard, meant that they set an extremely unfortunate example which was to blight the life and witness of many an Old Testament saint in succeeding centuries. The Lord tolerated polygamy under the Old Covenant but it is significant that all the polygamous situations referred to in Scripture, without exception, brought grief and unhappiness to those involved. The Bible's testimony is striking, although we should not be unduly surprised. Tearing up God's blueprint for marriage is bound to cause problems.

Spiritually speaking, their first error was in their failure to consult the Lord about the proposed course of action. There was no prayer for guidance, no seeking of his face or favour. Sarah has this bright idea from the best of motives. She takes it to Abraham and he appears immediately to agree to it. How typical this is of the way many of us so often behave! Matters are not developing as we believe the Lord wants. We start to get a little frustrated. It may be anything, from a purely personal matter to a concern for the lack of gospel success in our nation as a whole. We get to the point where we cry out, 'Lord, surely I have to do something!' So, with more planning than prayer, we devise all manner of schemes and programmes. They seem to be the answer. They seem to be such legitimate ways of fulfilling God's promises. Why, they even involve considerable self-sacrifice! But how often, as here, these plans and programmes of ours are doctrinally suspect and spiritually lacking. How vital it is, especially when we are feeling desperate, that we test every plan and project against the Word of God and in prayer.

The great lesson believers must learn is to wait for *the Lord* to remove whatever cross he lays upon us, in his own way and in his own time.

'His purposes will ripen fast,
Unfolding every hour;
The bud may have a bitter taste,
But sweet will be the flower.'[2]

It is, says the writer to the Hebrews, 'through faith and patience' that we 'inherit what has been promised' (6:12). It was ultimately through a lack of faith and patience that Abraham and Sarah involved themselves in this particular scheme.

Inevitably, a wrong course of action leads to further sin and misery. We read of Hagar that, 'When she knew she was pregnant, she began to despise her mistress. Then Sarai said to Abram, "You are responsible for the wrong I am suffering. I put my servant in your arms, and now that she knows she is pregnant, she despises me. May the LORD judge between you and me." "Your servant is in your hands," Abram said. "Do with her whatever you think best." Then Sarai ill-treated Hagar; so she fled from her' (Genesis 16:4-6).

Now none of the three protagonists emerges well from this mess, as passions run high. We have not seen Sarah in this mood before, but no doubt she is shouting at her husband at this stage. 'May the Lord judge,' she says. It is dangerous to invoke the Lord's judgement when tempers are raised. In such circumstances we always lose objectivity and, before we know it, we are back in Eden, shifting all the blame onto the next person. Sarah was at least partly responsible — it was her idea in the first place.

Abraham, on the other hand, despite the fact that he has now become Hagar's husband, refuses to accept any responsibility at all for the situation. 'It's nothing to do with me. She's your servant. You deal with her.' Such sin and misery could have been avoided had Abraham and Sarah exercised patience and faith rather than seeking to accelerate God's promise by taking matters into their own hands. Believers need to let the Lord remove his own cross, in his own time, in his own way.

If we step right back for a moment, we can see that the trouble probably started back in chapter 12, when Abraham's unfortunate response to the spiritual test of a famine was to leave the Promised Land for Egypt. It was presumably during this sad interlude that the household acquired the services of Hagar, who then accompanied them on their return to Canaan.

But if the wind had been sown, as far as this crisis was concerned, many years earlier, the whirlwind is being reaped even down to our own day. The descendants of Abraham and Hagar, the Arab nations, continue to fulfil the prophetic word spoken concerning them in this chapter: they 'will live in hostility towards all (their) brothers' (verse 12).

It is salutary to remember that great trouble can arise from sins committed out of the purest of motives and to realise that the Lord often takes the long view. Truly, with him, 'a thousand years are like a day' (2 Peter 3:8).

The Angel of the Lord

We come now to consider a unique and very moving theophany. Hagar flees in a turmoil of anger, pain, resentment and frustration. I do not think she is a true believer at this stage. Nor would her spiritual progress have been assisted by the treatment she had received at the hands of her master and mistress. How careful we need to be to maintain a credible Christian witness, especially to those who come into our homes.

From the fact that Hagar takes 'the road to Shur' (verse 7), it seems clear that she intended to return home to Egypt. There, by a spring in the desert, on the borders of that land, she rests wearily, filled with proud despair. Her attitude appears to be, 'By all the gods of Egypt, I would rather die than return to that man and that woman.' It is at that moment that the Lord appears to her.

I am sure, if the Lord were going to appear to us, we would prefer to be found in a spiritual frame of mind, just as we want to be alert and ready when the Saviour returns at the end of the age.[3] We certainly would not want to be in the grip of angry despair, the victim of a self-destructive fit of pique. That, nonetheless, was Hagar's sorry state when she experienced a theophany.

We read that, 'The angel of the LORD found Hagar near a spring in the desert' (Genesis 16:7). Here is the first reference to the Angel of the Lord in Scripture.[4] (Indeed, it is the first reference to *any* angel.) Occasionally, this key expression refers simply to an eminent member of the heavenly host who is in no way to be identified with God himself. The word 'angel' simply means 'messenger'. Most frequently, however, as is plainly indicated here, the Angel of the Lord is the preferred title of the Second Person of the Trinity when he appears in theophany.

Sometimes 'the Angel' clearly refers to God but is not seen. For example, in Chapter 21 of Genesis, he speaks to Hagar again but there is no theophany. We are distinctly told that, in this instance, 'The angel of God called to Hagar *from heaven*' (verse 17). She hears the Word of God but she does not see him. That is why we are considering this chapter but not that one. Genesis 16 records the only theophany in the experience of this woman.

Whenever the Son appears to a person as the Angel of the Lord, as he does particularly in the early history of Israel, it is an indication to us that Christ has come in his most human of forms, prior to the incarnation. He evidently looks so ordinary on such occasions that often the recipient of the glorious visit only slowly becomes aware of his true identity and nature. That is the case here.

His attitude towards her

What is most striking is the Lord's attitude towards Hagar. We read that the Lord had 'heard of' or, better, had just 'heard' her misery (verse 11). She had not prayed. Prayer was the last thing on her mind, certainly prayer to the God of Abraham. The Lord heard *her misery*; her very condition cried out to a tender God. What consolation that is to those too overwhelmed or too ignorant to pray. After all, she was not yet a true believer. She had neither the desire nor the ability to cry out to the Lord. Knowing that, the Father was prepared simply to hear her misery. How determined is our gracious God to find any excuse to rush to the aid of needy sinners!

She did not seek him, but we read those precious words, 'The angel of the LORD *found* Hagar' (verse 7), indicating that *he* had been seeking *her*. He is found by many who do not seek him. In this case, the Good

Shepherd finds his lost sheep in the wilderness, as, spiritually speaking, he often does. Even those of us who were conscious of crying out to an unknown God for help would gladly testify:

I sought the Lord and afterward I knew
He moved my soul to seek him from the start;
It was not I that found, O Saviour true;
No, you found out my heart.[5]

This gracious Saviour comes and calls Hagar by name (verse 8). His attitude towards his erring loved ones is always so intimate. Whenever I read this passage, it reminds me of the risen Lord's revelation of himself to that distraught woman who stood crying outside the tomb. He simply breathed her name, 'Mary', and so identified himself to her. Had Hagar been in the habit of having communion with her Lord, she too would then have known instantly who it was speaking to her.

Nonetheless, despite the loving and personal aspect of his greeting, the Son of God is not going to minimise the sinfulness of her situation. He is not prepared to call her Abraham's wife. That had never been his will. He calls her instead the 'servant of Sarai'. He always speaks to us as we really are, and not as we like to think of ourselves. When the Lord addresses us personally, he comes with a love that is both real *and* realistic, both exalting *and* humbling. 'Hagar, servant of Sarai.' We know the Lord is speaking to us when we are both lifted up and humbled at the same time. To those who have never known the personal call of God this must remain a paradox.

His timing with her

Consider now the Lord's timing with Hagar. 'The angel of the LORD found Hagar near a spring in the desert' (verse 7). Notice how he waits until her pride and resentment have to some extent burnt themselves out before he comes. He will often leave us until we are spent and exhausted. He waits a while so that we might see our folly. Then, as here, he very often stops us in our tracks. She was not expecting to see the Lord, let alone there and then. 'The Angel of the Lord found Hagar near a spring'. This 'spring' was in fact, we are told in verse 14, a 'well'.

We might easily be reminded of the occasion when the Lord met another sinful woman by a well. And was not his timing exquisite then, as he spoke to her of 'living water'?[6] Perhaps the Lord has led you out into a spiritual wilderness so that you will be meek and quiet and ready when the precise time comes for him to speak.

His questions to her

'And he said, "Hagar, servant of Sarai, where have you come from, and where are you going?"' (verse 8). The Lord gets straight down to business! Here are two questions that, from a spiritual perspective, all believers should be able to answer. 'Hagar, servant of Sarai, where have you come from?' Hagar, why are you running? Why are you fleeing from the place of duty and blessing, privilege and responsibility? Why run from about the only location on earth where the true God is honoured and worshipped? Why are you putting distance between yourself and the only place where you can find a spiritual sanctuary, and where your spiritual destiny will unfold? It is madness! Reconsider, before it is too late! 'Where have you come from?'

Hagar is like Onesimus, the slave who runs away from a Christian master, only to discover that he cannot outdistance the Lord.[7] You cannot run away from the Lord. He is everywhere. She is like the lost son in the famous story Jesus told, who had to run away to a 'distant country' before he 'came to his senses'.[8] Why did she flee? She fled, she said, because she could not bear to be so mistreated. How many leave the fold of the church for similar reasons. I can almost hear their complaints! Any pastor could list them.

The New Testament local church, like Abraham's household, is far from perfect. Sometimes members of the church family can be harsh and unloving. We can readily understand and have a lot of sympathy for Hagar as she runs away. But we also know that she was wrong to do so. Maybe, you are thinking about leaving your own fellowship because of the mistreatment you believe you have received. I might well sympathise with you as you pour out your story. Yet feelings of personal grievance, no matter how understandable, are very rarely sufficient reason for leaving a church.

At least Hagar is honest when answering the Lord's first question. When he says to her, 'Where have you come from?' she replies, 'I'm running away from my mistress Sarai' (verse 8). Well, precisely! Unwittingly perhaps, she condemns herself from her own mouth. If Sarah is legitimately her 'mistress', then she should not have deserted her. What duty, what responsibility, what cross might you be refusing to accept and bear? What are you running away from? Thank God the Saviour himself did not lay down his cross on the grounds that he deserved to be treated better! He might justly have done so, whereas, however unfairly we are dealt with, we deserve far worse. Because people have treated you badly, will you not obey God? That is a strange conclusion and you are on shaky ground, yet many go down that perilous path. Let us examine our own hearts.

When it comes to the second question, Hagar remains silent. 'Where are you going?' asks the Lord (verse 8). But she gives no answer, for she has no answer to give. She has no idea where she is going. She is fleeing to an unknown future. It is a leap in the dark. It is important to bear in mind that when the Lord asks questions, he never does so to increase our misery, but to restore us to himself. Hagar wants to avoid this question entirely and we often do the same. It is hard enough to look back, but calmly to examine the spiritual direction in which our lives are heading is often altogether too painful.

When the Lord met Hagar she was on the border that separated Egypt from the Promised Land. It was high time she considered the road she was taking. Did she really want to return to her old life of sin and idolatry? Were the treasures of Egypt really such adequate compensation for being out of the way of God's blessing? Is the Lord meeting you at a similarly critical juncture in your life?

His requirements of her

'Then the angel of the LORD told her, "Go back to your mistress and submit to her"' (Genesis 16:9). Such words falling from any other lips would seem unduly harsh. We might well imagine this would provoke some sharp retort. Instead she silently reflects on the Stranger's words. Perhaps, by this time, she is beginning to understand who it is who is speaking to her. She receives this command as from the Lord and takes no umbrage. Our natural instinct is to reject any rebuke we are given even when our conscience whispers that it might be merited. When, however, the Lord begins to soften our hearts, the calls he makes on us to repent begin to look remarkably like promises. The requirement implies help in its fulfilment. The stirrings of faith in Hagar's heart assure her of divine aid if she obeys the Angel of the Lord. She realises that he cannot be saying, 'Go back, and I will abandon you.' Whenever the Lord commands us to do something we know is right, we may be certain that his blessing will accompany our obedience.

The time would eventually come when it would be right for Hagar to leave Abraham's household,[9] but the time was not yet. There are occasions in all of our lives when the quaint-sounding words of a nineteenth century hymnwriter seem strangely compelling:

'Return, O wanderer, return,
And seek an injured Father's face;
Those warm desires that in thee burn
Were kindled by redeeming grace.'[10]

We must never make far-reaching decisions when our hearts are not right.

His promises concerning her

'The angel added, "I will so increase your descendants that they will be too numerous to count." The angel of the LORD also said to her: "You are now with child and you will have a son. You shall name him Ishmael, for the LORD has heard of your misery. He will be a wild donkey of a man; his hand will be against everyone and everyone's hand against him, and he will live in hostility towards all his brothers"' (Genesis 16:10-12). As suggested earlier, the prophecy in the final sentence speaks not so much of Ishmael personally but of his descendants, the Arab nations. But how merciful of God to encourage even while he rebukes! The apostle Paul always does something similar in his letters. We need to cultivate the same gracious pattern. How often the harsh words of Christians cut and wound when they profess to be spoken 'in love'.

Notwithstanding the greatness of the Lord's promises to Hagar, how much more wonderful are those the Lord makes to the repentant sinner today. We are urged to return with all the promises and consolations of the gospel.

'As surely as he overcame
And triumphed once for you,
So surely you that love His Name
Shall triumph in Him too.'[11]

Of course we shall, because God intends it to happen!

His effect upon her

'She gave this name to the LORD who spoke to her: "You are the God who sees me," for she said, "I have now seen the One who sees me." That is why the well was called Beer Lahai Roi; it is still there, between Kadesh and Bered' (Genesis 16:13-14).

Who was this Stranger who knew her name and who seemed to tell her everything she ever did as she sat beside the well?[12] She comes to her own conclusions, and she is right. The realisation dawns slowly, but in the end she is certain. She is filled with an awe and amazement that she is still alive. She is astonished at Christ's condescension towards her. All the time she had been in Abraham's household she had never seen him. She would never have expected to, though doubtless she heard of his appearances to her master. And now he manifests himself to her in the midst of her rebellion. What amazing grace!

Reading this account, how could any believer ever imagine that they are too far gone for the Lord to meet with them? If she ever thought at all, Hagar might have reflected, 'Well, I've burnt my boats with the God of Abraham. I almost believed in him at one time but now I've turned my back on him forever. In leaving God's servant Abraham, I have abandoned him as well. Even if he is the true God, he will want nothing to do with me now.'

If that is how she felt, Hagar's story proved her wrong. The Lord knew everything about her. He knew her rebellion, her resentment and pettiness. He knew what a poor, foolish, sinful woman she was — and yet he loved her and was determined to bless her, restore her and fill her with joy. And what he did for Hagar, he has done for countless others since.

'She gave this name to the LORD who spoke to her: "You are the God who sees me," for she said, "I have now seen the One who sees me."' What a profound effect this theophany has upon her. She speaks not of 'the God who sees *us*', in some general sense, but of 'the God who sees *me*'. She has felt something of the personal gaze of the Lord Jesus Christ. If only we were as impressed with this fact as was Hagar. He sees us always. He sees us everywhere. He not only sees us, he sees through us, unerringly, perfectly...

Moreover, when Hagar speaks of the Lord who 'sees' her, she means far more than we might think. When Scripture says, 'God hears' (and that incidentally is the meaning of the name Ishmael) it implies that he answers as well. So it is that 'God sees' means that he understands and is concerned. Hagar now knows what she has never previously suspected, that God cares for her.

It is often when feeling utterly alone and abandoned that God in his mercy reveals his compassion to us. Perhaps you sense you need exactly such a revelation of the Lord's loving kindness to you in your present circumstances. Remember, he loves to surprise us with his grace, just as he surprised Hagar. He longs to thrill and melt our dull, cold hearts.

A further effect of this theophany on Hagar is that it causes her to pray — and not to the gods of Egypt, but to the only true and living God. 'You are the God who sees me' may be fairly brief as prayers go, but it is a tremendous beginning to a life of prayer! Think of that dramatic moment when Christ revealed himself to Saul on the Damascus road. The same immediate effect is noted, 'Behold, he is praying' (Acts 9:11).[13] Whenever a Christian receives a fresh view of Jesus, it will lead inevitably to a revival in prayer. Some believers have admitted to me that they have not really prayed for a very long time. I might well turn them to this sixteenth chapter of Genesis. All we need is just a glimpse 'of the knowledge of the glory of God in the face of Christ' (2 Corinthians 4:6). Such a spiritual refreshing thaws out our frozen hearts and lips.

A sweet reunion

'So Hagar bore Abram a son, and Abram gave the name Ishmael to the son she had borne. Abram was eighty-six years old when Hagar bore him Ishmael' (Genesis 16:15-16). I would love to know the full story behind these final two verses! What is apparent is that Hagar returns and, as it is Abraham who names her son Ishmael, it is clear that he accepts both her and the astonishing tale she has to tell. This theophany has brought with it the grace of true repentance. For Hagar to have returned required great measures of humility, courage and faith. Most probably, though, she returned with joy in her heart at the prospect of speaking to Abraham of the One she had seen. We can only imagine what mutual confession, forgiveness and reconciliation took place in that godly household on her return. On the other hand, perhaps it is right to follow the example of Scripture and draw a veil over such a poignant scene. Let us simply close by saying, 'Where sin increased, grace increased all the more' (Romans 5:20).

Notes

1 1 Peter 3:5-6.

2 William Cowper, 'God moves in a mysterious way'.

3 Mark 13:32-37.

4 I am reminded of the mysterious verse in Hebrews that tells us we must 'not forget to entertain strangers, for by so doing some people have entertained angels without knowing it' (13:2). We may never receive the awesome shock experienced by some of these Old Testament characters but the thought is a grand incentive to genuinely Christian hospitality.

5 *The Pilgrim Hymnal,* 1904.

6 John 4:1-26.

7 Philemon

8 Luke 15:11-32

9 Genesis 21:14

10 William Bengo Collyer

11 **John Newton,** 'Rejoice, believer, in the Lord'.

12 Compare John 4:29

13 The NIV omits the here significant 'Behold'.

Shock treatment

Genesis 17

Genesis 17 is a chapter of immense significance because in it we are introduced to the rite of circumcision, the 'sign of the covenant' (verse 11) between Abraham and his God. Though we must at least glance at a subject of such importance, we are going to concentrate on the frequently neglected human aspects of the account, as Abraham's personal history unfolds. In this theophany, Abraham's fourth, the patriarch has to handle news that must have shaken him to the core of his being.

'When Abram was ninety-nine years old, the LORD appeared to him and said, "I am God Almighty; walk before me and be blameless"' (Genesis 17:1). We are not told the exact manner of his appearing but the Shekinah glory was clearly not totally concealed, as can be inferred from Abraham's reaction. We read in verse 3 that 'Abram fell face down'. This was not, in other words, God appearing in his most human form, as the Angel of the Lord. He had appeared as the Angel to Hagar in the previous chapter just as he would appear to Abraham once again in the next. Here in chapter 17, however, there is something very awesome in the revelation, a fact again borne out by the description of the Lord's departure. 'When he had finished speaking with Abraham, God *went up from him*' (verse 22). So here, the Son of God, though probably still assuming human form, does not conceal every visible aspect of his glory, the added reverence and solemnity this brought to the occasion being well in tune with its high purpose.

Yet, when I tell you that in this chapter Abraham receives one of the greatest shocks of his life, you are not to imagine that it was anything to do with the Lord's appearance. After all, this could hardly have been stranger than the theophany of Chapter 15. No, the great shock comes as the result of something that the Lord *says* to him; something the Lord adds to his main message, with an air of studied carelessness. What appears to be a throwaway remark is nevertheless designed to achieve the effect it certainly does, that of rocking Abraham back on his heels as never before.

The Covenant of Circumcision

To begin with, however, because it would surely be wholly inappropriate to discuss Genesis 17 without some explanation of the covenant of circumcision, let me interject some brief thoughts that may help to clarify our thinking. I am painfully aware that merely opening such a vast subject begs many questions but exploring covenant theology lies beyond the scope of this book!

Both the covenant, here confirmed by God, and the circumcision, which is the sign and the seal of that covenant, have two aspects. One aspect is natural, temporal, external and earthly; the other is spiritual, eternal, internal and heavenly. These two aspects can be simply demonstrated. Abraham is promised numerous descendants. The Lord said to him, 'I will confirm my covenant between me and you and will greatly increase your numbers' (Genesis 17:2). The natural, temporal, external, and earthly fulfilment of this covenant promise is to be found not only in the nation of Israel, but also in the many peoples who descended from Ishmael and from the sons of Abraham's third wife, Keturah.[1] In a purely natural and physical sense, Abraham was 'the father of many nations'.

The spiritual, eternal, internal and heavenly fulfilment of this promise is explained fully for us in the New Testament. There we are told 'Those who *believe* are the children of Abraham . . . . If you belong to Christ, then you are Abraham's seed, and heirs according to the promise' (Galatians 3:7, 29). What promise? Well, this promise, here in Genesis 17.

Similarly, as part of the covenant promise, Abraham and his descendants are promised the land. 'The whole land of Canaan, where you are now an alien, I will give as an everlasting possession to you and your descendants after you; and I will be their God' (Genesis 17:8). The natural, temporal, external and earthly fulfilment of this promise is clear. Eventually, the patriarch's natural descendants moved in to possess the land of Israel.

Equally clear is the spiritual, eternal, internal and heavenly aspect of this covenant promise. Abraham's spiritual seed, all true believers, have 'an inheritance' kept in heaven that, unlike the land, 'can never perish, spoil or fade' (1 Peter 1:4). It should not strike us as being unduly surprising therefore that circumcision, which is introduced here as the divinely ordained seal of God's covenant with Abraham, also displays these two aspects.

Circumcision sealed all the natural, temporal, external and earthly blessings for Abraham's descendants that accompanied outward obedience to the Law of Moses given to the nation of Israel on Mount Sinai. But circumcision also sealed spiritual, eternal, internal and heavenly blessings for all those whose living faith revealed them to be Abraham's seed in the deeper sense. To all such, circumcision was, in the words of the apostle Paul, 'A seal of the righteousness (they) had by faith' (Romans 4:11). This distinction points up the most vital of all differences between Old Testament (Covenant) Israel and the New Testament (Covenant) Church. Whereas the Old Covenant enclosed a spiritually mixed multitude, membership of the New Covenant depends on saving faith.

The prophet Jeremiah was looking forward to New Covenant days when he wrote, 'No longer will a man teach his neighbour, or a man his brother, saying, "Know the LORD," because *they will all know me,* from the least of them to the greatest," declares the LORD' (Jeremiah 31:34).[2] In Old Testament days, Abraham's *natural* children were circumcised as a sign that they had entered into the outward blessings of the Old Covenant. (It was, of course, to be hoped that eventually they would share Abraham's saving faith in the Messiah to come.) In New Testament days, Abraham's *spiritual* children are baptised as a sign that they have entered into the spiritual blessings of the New Covenant. There is a real analogy between Old Testament circumcision and New Testament baptism, but to baptise the *natural* children of believers is to misunderstand the essential distinction between the covenants.

I freely acknowledge that non-baptist reformed theologians—including Calvin—do not so neatly divide the covenant into natural and spiritual aspects and define the distinction between Old Covenant Israel and the New Covenant Church somewhat differently.

A Startling Revelation

The respective terms of the solemn agreement are carefully laid out: 'As for me. . .' (verse 4), 'As for you . . .' (verse 9). But then, instead of signing off after this very nicely balanced and rounded revelation of God, we have, it seems to me, a carefully contrived 'afterthought'.

"God *also* said to Abraham. . .' (In other words, 'Oh, by the way, Abraham, there is something else I might just mention . . .') 'As for Sarai your wife, you are no longer to call her Sarai; her name will be Sarah. I will bless her and will surely give you a son by her. I will bless her so that she will be the mother of nations; kings of peoples will come from her' (Genesis 17:15 and 16).

Let me explain why this came to Abraham as one of the biggest shocks of his life. That it was a shock is very clear from his immediate reaction. First of all, we read he 'fell face down' (verse 17). As he had already fallen face down at the first appearance of the Son of God (verse 3), I conclude that Abraham simply rises to his feet in sheer astonishment as he hears these words, only to fall prostrate once again as soon as he remembers himself. And then he laughs (verse 17), and we shall try and see exactly what lay behind this rather incongruous reaction a little later.

Abraham is obviously in deep shock as he hears these words. To find out precisely why, we need to be aware of his state of heart and mind. Thirteen years have elapsed since Hagar's return home and the birth of Ishmael. No great mathematical genius is required to work that out. In the last verse of chapter 16, Abraham is eighty-six years old and in the first verse of chapter 17 he is ninety-nine. You will recall that it was because Sarah had not been specifically named as the mother of Abraham's progeny that, with the best of motives, she had suggested the marriage to her maidservant, Hagar.

When the pregnant Hagar returns from her flight and announces that she has seen the Lord and he has promised that the descendants of her unborn child will be 'too numerous to count' (Genesis 16:10), Abraham and Sarah very naturally jump to the wrong conclusion. They naturally assume that this is the Lord's vindication of the course of action they have taken to ensure that Abraham's line will be continued.

What greater confirmation could have been given? How gladly Abraham names the new-born child Ishmael, 'God hears'! How gracious God has been to reassure them in this wonderful way, so dispelling any qualms or uneasiness they might have otherwise felt! Peace and joy are restored to the household as further proof that all is in accordance with the perfect will of God. . .

So it is that, for the following thirteen years, a remarkable and unreal situation prevails. Abraham, Sarah and Hagar all believe Ishmael to be the child of promise through whom God's covenant commitment to Abraham will be fulfilled, when, in fact, he is not. The implications of any significant, long-term misreading of divine guidance are always complex and traumatic. The moment when such realisation dawns on the believer will inevitably prove immensely difficult. No wonder the Lord's seemingly casual 'afterthought' leaves Abraham groping to understrand how the words he is hearing can be reconciled with all his long-cherished expectations and assumptions.

Spiritual stagnation

Abraham and Sarah should have realised that their attempt to fulfil God's promise was quite wrong, but they misread circumstances and were consequently confirmed in their error. Something tragically similar occurs in the lives of many Christian believers. With the very best of intentions, they take a wrong decision and a false direction. As in this case, there is no prayerful consideration, nor is any proposed course of action tested by God's revealed Word. What spiritual danger we invite and what heartache we so easily lay up for ourselves for the future when we neglect these basic precautions and rely only on human reasoning.

The error is often compounded when providence, that most unreliable of guides, seems to smile on the solution and completely dispels any sense of uneasiness there might initially have been.

What is the result? In the case of Abraham and Sarah it was thirteen wasted years of spiritual stagnation, during which, as far as we can tell, the Lord never really spoke to them at all. If we were to ask, 'Well, why didn't they notice that?' the answer would be because they had become spiritually complacent. Their whole spiritual problem stemmed from their conviction that they had already received what God had promised them. They were no longer earnestly seeking the Lord. Up until that time, their persistent cry had been, 'Lord, when are you going to honour your word?' After the birth of Ishmael, however, we can readily imagine how the spiritual climate of the household would alter. Everything now appears to be sewn up. The desperate need to wait upon the Lord and discover his will and purpose for them has been dissipated completely. Spiritual complacency sets in. After all, do they not now possess the most important thing the Lord had to give them?

What an awful state to be in! The most serious spiritual conditions are usually those of which we are unaware. The worst of all must be when believers are actually deluded into imagining they are receiving the blessing of God. The result is spiritual stagnation that may last for years. Could somebody reading these words have fallen into this trap? I do not know what spiritual mistakes you made, nor what circumstance confirmations you received that led you into such a sorry state. It hardly matters any more. My prayer is simply that the Lord Jesus Christ, in his infinite grace, will come to you again as he did to Abraham, even though you no longer really seek his face.

He comes to Abraham in great love, but not without a gentle rebuke. 'When Abram was ninety-nine years old, the LORD appeared to him and said, "I am God Almighty; walk before me and be blameless"' (Genesis 17:1). I would interpret the Lord's words like this: 'Walk before *me*, Abraham, not Sarah, don't walk before *her*. Walk before me and be blameless, *as once you were*. What has been happening over these past few years? Have you become so spiritually deadened that you are unaware of the distance that has grown up between us? Can it really be that you have not missed that living and vital relationship that once we shared? Is it possible? Surely, Abraham, you sensed that something was wrong!'

Well, perhaps he had. Perhaps you do, as well. It still, however, takes the gracious intervention of a loving Saviour to dispel such spiritual complacency and to resurrect long-dead expectations and desires. Thankfully, he is not content to let his followers settle for second-best solutions and eagerly disturbs any unwarranted peace of mind.

Restored to simple faith

There are some people the Lord is so impatient to see back in true fellowship and service that he is not prepared to restore them slowly. There are times when, apparently, only shock treatment will do. I have seen careless and somewhat wordly church members suddenly transformed, becoming alert once again to their spiritual responsibilities, eager once more to live for their Master. They have had a shock to their system. Somehow the Lord has broken in on their spiritual reverie and said, 'Hey! You've worked your life out all wrong! I am going to use and bless you in ways you gave up imagining were possible years ago!'

That is exactly what the Son of God is saying to Abraham here. 'As for Sarai your wife, you are no longer to call her Sarai; her name will be Sarah. I will bless her and will surely give you a son by her. I will bless her so that she will be the mother of nations; kings of peoples will come from her' (Genesis 17:15-16).

Notice Abraham's reaction. 'Abraham fell face down; he laughed and said to himself, "Will a son be born to a man a hundred years old? Will Sarah bear a child at the age of ninety?"' (verse 17). He laughs. Now a laugh can mean many things. Is this a laugh of despair or of joy? Does it express faith or doubt? Sometimes people laugh when they do not know how to react. A laugh may well indicate a very complex and undecided reaction that may include embarrassment, confusion, amazement, sheer incomprehension, or all these things mixed together.

There is nothing funny happening here; but Abraham laughs. I have tried to imagine the turmoil of emotion that must have swept over him like a great wave as he fought to take in what the Lord was saying. No doubt, also, riding on the back of the wave, was a rapidly growing recognition of the irony of it all. 'Will a son be born to a man a hundred years old? Will Sarah bear a child at the age of ninety?' It is not difficult to guess Abraham's unspoken thoughts. 'Surely you are not telling me I have to go back to believing that! Lord, we found another way, remember? We were all so relieved when Ishmael was born. You told us to call him 'God hears'. You appeared to Hagar and made the same promises to her as you had to me. No, please Lord, no! It was hard enough to believe that Sarah and I could have a son thirteen years ago, how can I believe it now? How do I tell Sarah and Hagar? What do I tell the boy — "I'm sorry, son, we've all made a dreadful mistake. You are not the child of promise we have raised you to be all these years"?'

So the patriarch makes one last feeble effort to steer the Lord round to a more 'reasonable' path: 'And Abraham said to God, "If only Ishmael might live under your blessing!"' (Genesis 17:18). Have you ever tried this kind of approach with the Lord? 'Lord, let's just be reasonable for a moment here. We have this boy and he's a fine lad. I've brought him up to know, respect and trust you. In fact, this Ishmael is everything anybody could want. Let's not waste thirteen years, Lord! Let's use him! Let him be the one!' With somewhat bated breath, we wait to see how the Lord will respond. Has Abraham finally pushed the Saviour's patience an inch too far?

'Then God said, "Yes, but your wife Sarah will bear you a son, and you will call him Isaac. I will establish my covenant with him as an everlasting covenant for his descendants after him. And as for Ishmael, I have heard you: I will surely bless him; I will make him fruitful and will greatly increase his numbers. He will be the father of twelve rulers, and I will make him into a great nation. But my covenant I will establish with Isaac, whom Sarah will bear to you by this time next year"' (Genesis 17:19-21).

Perhaps it would be better to replace the NIV's 'Yes, but' with the straight 'No' of other versions in verse 19. The Lord knows what Abraham has in mind! He is happy to confirm that Ishmael will receive much material blessing but nevertheless quietly and firmly re-states in no uncertain terms that it is to be through Sarah and her son, who is to be called Isaac, that his covenant will be established. Abraham senses the struggle between his own preconceptions and wishes and the will of God. We can all identify with him there. Sooner or later, we all face that struggle and sometimes it is very fierce and painful. But the gracious nature of the Lord's reply to Abraham assures us that we may unburden ourselves to him without any fear that we might anger him.

How easy it is to end up in a spiritual cul-de-sac because some time in the past we bowed to expediency rather than waiting on God to reveal his way. What complications we bring into our lives as a result!

Maybe there is some basic truth or promise of God that you have not been able to accept or trust. Somebody then gave you a clever way of avoiding the problem altogether and you eagerly grabbed it. Now, though you are at a spiritual standstill, the Lord is waking you up to the fact and telling you to believe that truth or promise in the simple and obvious way you know was always intended. What are you to do? You have no reason to be afraid to go to the Lord and unburden yourself of this whole matter. You can go to him and be absolutely assured that you will not overstretch his patience. He would not have spoken to you at all if he were not prepared to respond in grace and mercy. Get all your fears and concerns sorted out, so that you may once more know the delights of undiluted joy in trusting and serving Christ.

New names

Although we have always referred to 'Abraham' and 'Sarah' when not directly quoting Scripture, it is during this theophany that they receive these familiar names. The 'exalted father' (Abram) becomes the 'father of many' (Abraham), while the 'princess' (Sarai and Sarah) has her name slightly amended, perhaps to emphasise its significance. The meaning of the names, however, is probably not as important as the fact that they were changed. New names signal a new beginning, a fresh start for two rather elderly people.

In Revelation 3:12 we read, 'Him who overcomes I will make a pillar in the temple of my God. Never again will he leave it. I will write on him the name of my God and the name of the city of my God, the New Jerusalem, which is coming down out of heaven from my God; and I will also write on him my new name.' The Lord loves fresh starts, and often in the Bible they are indicated by the giving of new names. Most wonderful of all, his people will share in *his* 'new name' which assures them of the ultimate enjoyment of the glory of the Son of God.

Is it possible to be restored to what we were? Can we really get back to that point where somehow we went astray? May simple faith be restored and wrong relationships put right, even after a long period of backsliding?

The answer is 'Yes' because of a third 'new' name in Genesis 17. Actually, it occurs in the very first verse, 'When Abram was ninety-nine years old, the LORD appeared to him and said, "I am God Almighty."' This is the first occurrence in the Bible of that great title of God, El Shaddai. There have been many attempts to translate and explain its meaning. Essentially, it suggests a God who is full of power; an all-sufficient God of wonders, who is able to perform the most amazing miracles. As the hymnwriter puts it: 'Ponder anew what the Almighty can do'.[3] El Shaddai. 'What is impossible with man is possible with God' (Luke 18:27).

I love to read the proof of this in verse 23: '*On that very day* Abraham took his son Ishmael and all those born in his household or bought with his money, every male in his household, and circumcised them, as God told him.' In fact, Abraham himself was circumcised 'on that same day' (verse 26). There is a commentary on this passage in Romans 4, where Paul remarks, 'Without weakening in his faith, he faced the fact that his body was as good as dead — since he was about a hundred years old — and that Sarah's womb was also dead. Yet he did not waver through unbelief regarding the promise of God, but was strengthened in his faith and gave glory to God, being fully persuaded that God had power to do what he had promised' (verses 19-21). Those words were written in response to the events we have been considering. Though Abraham's understanding of the situation had been awry for thirteen years, the very instant he was certain of God's correction, his faith was completely redirected.

The test was enormous and might well have precipitated a terrible spiritual crisis. How many would have handled it with such calm and holy resignation? The struggle is momentary. There is this brief request regarding Ishmael, and then within minutes, this great and godly man has recomposed himself, totally reorientated his thinking, and begun to put the Lord's commands into effect. Amazingly, it appears, as Paul declared, he 'was strengthened in his faith and gave glory to God'. The closing verses of Genesis 17 provide a tremendous testimony to the courage and faith of this man Abraham. What an example to those who would claim to be his spiritual children!

Notes

1. Genesis 25:1-4.
2. See also Hebrews 8.
3. See chapter 4, note 6.

A faith restored

Genesis 18:1-15

Genesis 18 is quite simply one of the most remarkable chapters in the Bible. From the point of view of theophany, no one who knows and loves the Lord Jesus Christ of the New Testament could fail to recognise him here.

This particular theophany is perhaps unique in that it is extended to fulfil two quite separate purposes, purposes that appear at first sight to be almost contradictory the one to the other. Yet, for the Lord Jesus Christ, it is clearly an effortless transition from the wonderfully tender promise of redemption in verses 1-15 to the chilling announcement of judgment that overshadows the rest of the chapter. It is sobering to reflect on the fact that though God loves mercy, he is also glorified in the death of the wicked.

This encounter with the Son of God takes place very shortly after the events of chapter 17.[1] Abraham has recovered from the great shock that he received on that occasion. He has come to terms with the thirteen years spent in the spiritual wilderness during which he had mistakenly imagined that Ishmael was the child of promise. But Abraham must nevertheless have been far from happy, because Sarah, as we shall see, had not been able to make the adjustment to these radically altered circumstances. This surely grieved the heart of the great man.

When a husband and a wife cannot press forward together in true spiritual union there is always much sadness and consternation. In actual fact, it was precisely in order to prevent a potentially serious rift developing between this godly couple, Abraham and Sarah, that the Angel of the Lord and his two angelic companions presented themselves outside Abraham's tent 'near the great trees of Mamre . . . in the heat of the day' (Genesis 18:1).

But before we arrive at the main purpose of this part of the theophany, let us first glance at the mere social formalities of the occasion, which are in themselves beautifully instructive.

A meal to remember

'The LORD appeared to Abraham near the great trees of Mamre while he was sitting at the entrance to his tent in the heat of the day. Abraham looked up and saw three men standing nearby. When he saw them, he hurried from the entrance of his tent to meet them and bowed low to the ground. He said, "If I have found favour in your eyes, my lord, do not pass your servant by. Let a little water be brought, and then you may all wash your feet and rest under this tree. Let me get you something to eat, so you can be refreshed and then go on your way — now that you have come to your servant." "Very well," they answered, "do as you say." So Abraham hurried into the tent to Sarah. "Quick," he said, "get three seahs of fine flour and knead it and bake some bread." Then he ran to the herd and selected a choice, tender calf and gave it to a servant, who hurried to prepare it. He then brought some curds and milk and the calf that had been prepared, and set these before them. While they ate, he stood near them under a tree' (Genesis 18:1-8).

It is siesta time and Abraham has been deep in thought, perhaps puzzling over how he might get through to Sarah. The radical realignment of his thinking produced by his recent encounter with the Lord has been greeted with utter horror and disbelief. He is at a loss to know how to encourage his wife to join him in the renewal of this great endeavour of faith. It would be hardly surprising if the strain on their relationship had not given rise to a distinctly frosty atmosphere . . .

Suddenly he looks up and is startled to see three strangers standing nearby. Where had they come from? How had they arrived so silently? Bear in mind that it only gradually dawns upon Abraham that his principal guest is none other than the Lord. This is no great cause for wonder. At least during recent appearances, the Lord has revealed himself to Abraham to some extent or other in a glorified form. But now, in his last true theophany, he is privileged to share fellowship with the Saviour almost as though he were a New Testament apostle.

Anyway, whether or not Abraham recognised anything unusual in the appearance of these 'men', to begin with he certainly 'entertained angels without knowing it' (Hebrews 13:2).[2] Especially was he unaware that one of them was the Angel of the Lord. He simply offered hospitality in the same way as he would have done to any travellers. Yet it is often in the automatic, routine responses of life that our true character is revealed. Abraham here had no desire to impress and no thought of gain and so the stature of the man is all the more tellingly displayed.

Most men in his position would have exhibited an understandable pride. Not so, Abraham. He was considered a great man in the area, being extremely wealthy with many servants and much livestock. The local kings were in his debt. Undoubtedly, Abraham had become a highly respected, if not revered, regional dignitary. Nonetheless, this great man bows low to these strangers in genuinely unaffected humility. This is, we sense, far more than a mere formal greeting, simply a custom of the times. Gladly he stands by while they are eating, eager to assist them in any way. Notice also the alacrity with which he goes about this hospitality. He hurries to greet his guests (verse 2) and hurries to meet their needs (verse 6). He runs to select 'a choice, tender calf' and, because such urgency is catching, his servant hurries to prepare it (verse 7)!

Then we cannot help but comment on the lavishness of this hospitality. We are told that he offers 'something to eat' in verse 5. Literally, he begs them to receive 'a little bread'. And yet this 'little bread' turns out to be a sumptuous meal. It reminds me of the times I go to Northern Ireland and am offered 'a wee bite' in every Christian home, regardless of the time of day, and the table groans with all manner of delicious, high-calorie food! Every aspect of Abraham's kindness towards total strangers who were never likely to repay him provides us with a model to follow.

What fails to come out very clearly in verse 5 in the NIV is the fact that he recognises that providence has brought them to him. He says, virtually, 'This is why you have come to me, to receive this hospitality.' The implication is that, as their arrival is plainly part of God's will, they have no need to thank him. He is simply doing what God would have him do.

New Testament echoes

A number of Scriptures come into my mind as I reflect on this lovely scene. I think of the Lord Jesus in the upper room, after he has washed his disciples' feet, saying, 'If anyone loves me, he will obey my teaching. My Father will love him, and we will come to him and make our home with him' (John 14:23). How touching is this wonderful illustration of that promise. Abraham's loving obedience is being graciously recognised at the outset of this last meeting on earth between him and his Saviour.

I am also reminded of the words of the glorified Christ to those Christians at Laodicea whose spiritual complacency had rendered their faith dangerously 'low.' 'Here I am! I stand at the door and knock. If anyone hears my voice and opens the door, I will come in and eat with him, and he with me' (Revelation 3:20). When the Son of God deigned to eat Abraham's food, he was acknowledging the end of the patriarch's thirteen years of spiritual inertia. Then again, I recall how Jesus similarly made himself known during a meal in a house in the village of Emmaus.[3] I am led on to consider how often the Lord to this day reveals himself spiritually to believers as they meet, according to his command, to eat and drink at the Lord's Supper.

This episode in Genesis 18 can also be viewed as a literal fulfilment of Jesus' words on the Day of Judgement, 'For I was hungry and you gave me something to eat, I was thirsty and you gave me something to drink, I was a stranger and you invited me in' (Matthew 25:35). Yet is it not our privilege to be able to do precisely the same? For whatever we do for the least of our brothers and sisters in Christ, we do for him (Matthew 25:40). Hospitality is a great and necessary Christian grace and one that is highly productive of fruit for God's kingdom.

The New Testament verse that comes home to me most of all as I read this passage, however, is found in the letter of James: '"Abraham believed God and it was credited to him as righteousness," and he was called God's friend' (James 2:23). What more wonderful title could Abraham possibly have? Twice he is called 'God's friend' in the Old Testament[4] and James rightly considers it remarkable enough to mention, seeing the friendship of God as the reward of faith.

The very human nature of this theophany is surely a gracious reward for the amazing way in which Abraham was prepared in chapter 17 almost instantly to abandon his long-cherished misconceptions concerning Ishmael and simply believe the Word of God.

The lesson we may safely draw is that whoever demonstrates such faith-induced flexibility will surely enjoy the same intensely intimate fellowship with the Lord that God's friend, Abraham, was granted on this occasion.

Why Christ appeared

We now come to consider the main reason for this appearance. Sarah had not been able to recover the simple faith in God's promise that once she had possessed. She *should* have believed. No doubt Abraham had shared the staggering news that she was even yet to have a son by him, but Sarah is quite unable to receive it. She felt perhaps that Abraham was deluded or, worse, that God himself was playing games with them both. At times it may well have been that she pretended to believe, for her husband's sake. It is unlikely, however, that Abraham was fooled for a moment.

He sits 'at the entrance to his tent in the heat of the day', longing that Sarah could truly share in his joy and expectancy. He thinks to himself, 'I suppose I shall just have to wait until the time comes', but God has other plans. So miraculous and so significant was the birth of Isaac to be that the Lord was not prepared to bring it to pass without *both* parents being spiritually attuned and fully in fellowship with him. Hence the reason for this fascinating theophany.

In Hebrews 11:11 we read, 'By faith even Sarah herself received ability to conceive, even beyond the proper time of life, since she considered him faithful who had promised.'[5] God decided that such was the overwhelming significance of this impending birth that it would be quite unfitting for Sarah to conceive Isaac without Abraham's faith. Therefore, having made faith a condition of this miracle, he had to come and kindle that faith in Sarah's heart.

Maybe you are finding it especially difficult to believe the promises of God for his people, and for yourself in particular, at this time. Let me therefore simply outline the way in which, with divine sensitivity, the Lord Jesus Christ restores Sarah's faith. Then perhaps, as we do so, you will recognise that your Saviour is operating in a somewhat similar way with you.

Obviously, the Lord *returns in a special way*. 'The LORD appeared to Abraham near the great trees of Mamre while he was sitting at the entrance to his tent in the heat of the day. Abraham looked up and saw three men standing nearby' (Genesis 18:1-2). It has been a long time, thirteen years, since Sarah had been close to the Lord. Now he comes to her in this rather oblique manner and in a guise that even her husband was slow to recognise.

The Lord may well employ exceptional means in order to fix our attention once more fully on him after a period of alienation from him. Sometimes the Lord approaches us in the strangest of ways, which are nevertheless perfectly adapted to reach us. He may go to extraordinary lengths just so that we may hear his voice, even though we are far from inclined to listen. As the story unfolds, we begin to appreciate how the circumstances of this theophany were tailor-made for the purpose of transforming a woman who protected her battered and weak faith with a veneer of cynicism. Whatever our condition, 'God does not take away life; instead, he devises ways so that a banished person may not remain estranged from him' (2 Samuel 14:14).

Restoration underway

In this case, the first thing the Lord does is he *receives her service*. 'Abraham hurried into the tent to Sarah. "Quick," he said, "get three seahs of fine flour and knead it and bake some bread"' (Genesis 18:6). The Lord eats the bread that Sarah bakes. He has come to minister to her, but first of all he allows her to minister to him. It is often an effective way of building bridges with unbelievers, allowing them to assist you in some practical matter or leisure pursuit. It is a lovely tactic that the Lord often employs when he seeks to restore the flagging faith of his people.

Perhaps, though your faith has been burning low, the Lord has encouraged and enabled you in recent days to pray and worship him with a reality that you have not experienced in a long time. Or maybe you have been drawn to perform some helpful act of Christian love on behalf of some needy fellow-believer. Remember, that is serving the Lord, as well. But whatever it has been, somewhere in the process you have become dimly aware, for the first time in ages, that you have actually been doing something for Christ's sake. It has not been just an act of human kindness; it has been a *godly* act you have been engaged in. You have been constrained. The Lord planted the desire in your heart and then gave you the strength to do it. It may have been a very little thing. It was a little thing for Sarah to bake some bread. Why, she could have done that for anybody, but the Lord made sure she did it for him. In such simple ways, the Lord may reestablish fellowship with himself and begin to restore faith.

There are further indications that the Saviour *respects her frailty*. The brief ninth verse is remarkably rich: '"Where is your wife Sarah?" they asked him. "There in the tent," he said.' Now, of course, we know not only that Sarah is eavesdropping (verse 10) but that the Lord is fully aware of the fact. Picture the scene; it is by no means devoid of humour.

In what I imagine was probably a slightly louder voice than would have been needed purely for Abraham's benefit, the Son of God asks this key question, 'Where is your wife Sarah?' Before we look at its significance, let us not miss the gentleness of Christ in all of this. Even though he has appeared in his most human form, as the Angel of the Lord, to have confronted Sarah directly would have intimidated her beyond measure. It would have been beyond what she could possibly have borne in her present spiritual state. That is why he speaks to her through Abraham.

This seems to me so helpful and so typical of the way the Lord often works when he wants to restore faith. Instead of speaking directly through his Word, which may not be being opened anyway, he chooses to speak to us indirectly. It may be through a friend or family member; it could be that the words of a hymn or song suddenly strike home. Maybe some unusual event or sad providence brings us up short or we are stirred up by some sudden memory. The means the Lord might use are practically endless.

How gently the Lord deals with us! We must be just as tender when dealing with those whose spiritual appetite is small. Some kind word or act, even simply a genuinely accepting attitude, may be just the instrument that God will use to restore their hunger for him. We need great wisdom to know how to approach friends who have grown cold or cynical. It is not always right to be direct. Despite appearances, this theophany is not for Abraham's benefit. It *will* be towards the end of chapter 18, but not now. This is all for Sarah, though she is far from realising it.

It could be that you are idly flicking through the pages of this book as you read these words. You have long since given up any serious study of the Bible and your faith is at an all time low. The Lord may stop you in your tracks even now. He knows how to reach you, 'for he knows how we are formed, he remembers that we are dust' (Psalm 103:14).

Self examination

The next thing we find is that the Saviour *requires her self-examination*. This is the main point of the inquiry in the ninth verse. Whenever, during a theophany, the Lord asks this type of question, it is never geographical, always spiritual. 'Where are you?' the Lord Jesus Christ calls to Adam in the Garden of Eden (Genesis 3:9). 'Where have you come from and where are you going?' the Lord Jesus Christ asks Hagar by the well in the desert (Genesis 16:8). 'Where is your wife Sarah?' he asks Abraham here.

Now there does not appear to have been any small talk during the meal. We get the impression it was conducted in silence, with Abraham looking on. That being so, it would make the Stranger's opening words all the more startling. 'Where is your wife Sarah?' Abraham must have been completely taken aback. This was not the sort of question that a casual traveller in the desert would ask his host. In fact, it was a real shocker, because etiquette demanded that no reference be made to the women of the household, let alone that they should be enquired after by name! 'Where is your wife Sarah?' Here are the first clues to Abraham that this is no ordinary guest. He thinks to himself, 'Who is this man who knows my wife's name and asks after her as though they are acquainted?'

As for Sarah, she must almost have fallen through the tent-flap! But as the question raced round her mind, it began to do its searching work. Where *was* she? What was the state of her heart? How was she coping? What was going on? Has the Lord suddenly caused you to examine your own heart in recent days, to reflect on how far you may be from him? If so, he is clearing the ground of rubble in preparation for rebuilding your faith. The Saviour always comes with gracious purposes. He does not come to mock you. He comes as the good Shepherd, longing to find his lost and wandering sheep. He asks us to consider just where we stand before him.

At this stage, in order to revive Sarah's memory, the Lord *repeats his promises*. She has heard the promise about the son that is going to be born many, many times over many, many years. Up until now, however, she has always heard it second hand. The Lord had always appeared to Abraham and the fact that he eventually appeared to Hagar went a long way to convincing Sarah that the promise was being fulfilled without her.

Now, just when she needs it most, she hears the promise for the first time from the Lord's own lips. And she hears it stated not only once but twice. 'I will surely return to you about this time next year, and Sarah your wife will have a son' (verse 10). Then, even after she has laughed in disbelief, the Saviour again declares, 'I will return to you at the appointed time next year and Sarah will have a son' (verse 14). There can be no possibility of Sarah claiming to have misheard!

Have the very promises which *you* have found so hard to believe sounded again and again with a peculiar intensity of late? Perhaps you have doubted that most foundational of all promises, the one that says, 'to us a child is born, to us a son is given' (Isaiah 9:6). I remember a man who came to four or five Christmas services where the great truth of the incarnation of God was repeatedly proclaimed. At the end, he remarked, 'The Lord kept on telling me until I believed it.' The Saviour did exactly that for Sarah. He may well do the same for you. Then you will believe the promises because they will not be coming to you second hand.

A laugh of disbelief

The good intentions of the Saviour towards Sarah are further underlined when we understand that he *recognises her graces*. 'So Sarah laughed to herself as she thought, "After I am worn out and my master is old, will I now have this pleasure?"' (Genesis 18:12). Even in the midst of all her doubt and disbelief the Lord finds something to commend. Not that he did so openly at the time. We have to wait 2,000 years to discover what it was.

The apostle Peter was writing his first letter, and the Holy Spirit caused him to reflect upon Sarah and what a tremendous wife she had been. So Peter held her up as a model and declared that Christian wives should be submissive to their husbands, like Sarah, 'who obeyed Abraham and called him her master' (1 Peter 3:6). As this is the only occasion in the biblical record when Sarah does call her husband 'master', Peter must have been thinking of Genesis 18. The most remarkable thing is that the Holy Spirit finds something to commend in a comment full of cynical derision and rank disbelief!

Does this not convince us that in the midst of all our doubts and sorrows, in the midst even of our sin, the Lord is concerned to find something he might acclaim? Is that not comforting? The Lord longs to uncover the slightest marks of grace, wherever they might appear. What greater evidence could there be of the Lord's merciful intentions towards us? What an excellent restorative for faith.

As a further encouragement towards Sarah's spiritual rehabilitation, he *reveals his omniscience* to her. 'Then the LORD said to Abraham, "Why did Sarah laugh and say, 'Will I really have a child, now that I am old?'"' (Genesis 18:13). It is at this point that any remaining vestige of doubt about the Stranger's identity is removed: 'Then the LORD said . . .' From now on, we may safely assume that Abraham at least has become fully aware that he is being granted a peculiarly intimate theophany. Who else but God could detect the inaudible, inward laugh of a concealed person? Jesus reveals himself as the omniscient searcher of hearts. How appropriate are the words of the apostle John, when he said of Jesus, 'He knew what was *in* a man' (John 2:25). Sarah was anxious not to reveal her presence and so she only 'laughed to herself' (verse 12), but immediately the searcher of hearts responds and asks, 'Why did Sarah laugh?'

I suppose Abraham looked a little nonplussed, knowing nothing of Sarah's laugh, nor even that she was listening. The Lord knows far more about us than even our nearest and dearest. He understands what motivates those doubts and fears that even a loving wife or husband cannot really fathom. He wants us to know that we cannot fool him, and that it is foolish to try. He wants us to know that, in seeking to restore our faith, he will reject everything that is sham and superficial. There is no point in pretending. He knows our hearts.

The restoration process continues as the Son of God *reassures her of his omnipotence*, with one of the most oft-quoted questions that we find in the Bible: 'Is anything too hard for the LORD?' (Genesis 18:14). Literally, 'Is anything too *wonderful* for the LORD?' When we are told in Isaiah 9:6 that the Son who is being given to us 'will be called Wonderful', the same word is used. I often say to people, 'If you can believe the first verse in the Bible, you can believe all that follows it.' Or, if you can believe that God is the One who can bring the dead back to life, then nothing else should give you a problem. Is anything too hard, too wonderful for the Lord? The question answers itself. If he truly is the God of the Bible, then the answer must be a resounding 'No!'

As the angel Gabriel told Mary when he announced that she was to bear not just an Isaac but the Messiah himself, 'Nothing is impossible with God' (Luke 1:37). When faith is burning low, there can be no more direct remedy than to be convinced of this. Nothing is impossible with God. Nothing.

No excuse allowed

Faith requires the security of knowing where the boundaries are. That is why the treatment of her unbelief is not complete until the Lord *rebukes her self-justification*. 'Sarah was afraid, so she lied and said, "I did not laugh." But he said, "Yes, you did laugh"' (Genesis 18:15). It makes *me* want to laugh when I think of this disembodied voice suddenly floating out from behind the tent-flap! I like to imagine her hand flying to her mouth as soon as she has said it. Her comment was the produce of sinful instinct. 'I didn't laugh.' But the retort from the Lord is swift and decisive. 'Oh, yes you did laugh. Let's not have any of that!' (Meanwhile, Abraham has completely lost the plot and is beginning to understand that this theophany is not primarily for him!)

Perhaps, momentarily, Sarah really thought she had not laughed, but she is immediately forced to confront the true state of her heart. The Saviour's response is amazingly gentle when we consider her double sin, unbelief compounded with untruth.

I am sure I recognise here the Jesus who, while reaching out his hand to Peter, as the disciple began to sink beneath the stormy waves of the Sea of Galilee, lamented, "You of little faith, why did you doubt?" (Matthew 14:31). He will not allow us to excuse our spiritual state, because he wants our spiritual state to be lifted. He will not let us get away for a moment with thinking that maybe we are all right spiritually when that is far from being the case. He is not content, even if we are, for us to continue living at a miserable, faithless, sub-Christian level. He wants something so much better for us. He cuts through our pretence and exposes our attempts at self-justification. Once we are prepared to confess our plight and our need of divine help, then he says, 'Now let me lift you up. Now let me give you real faith. Now let me infuse the grace and strength into your life you so desperately need.' He will not allow us to excuse our spiritual state but neither will he break the bruised reed or snuff out the smouldering wick.[6] Let us confess our unbelief, if there is any in our hearts. Let us repent of it. Sarah did, and proved that 'everything is possible for (her) who believes' (Mark 9:23).

Notes

1 Compare Genesis 17:21 and 18:10.

2 It seems clear that this incident was in the mind of the writer to the Hebrews.

3 Luke 24:13-35.

4 2 Chronicles 20:7 and Isaiah 41:8.

5 New American Standard Version. Most translations follow suit, while the NIV takes a different line, in an admittedly problematic verse.

6 Matthew 12:20.

Pleading for Sodom

Genesis 18:16-33

Once the Son of God had restored Sarah's faith with such divine tenderness and imagination, Abraham fully expected him, along with his two angelic companions, suddenly to disappear. After all, that was what had happened at the end of previous encounters. He was therefore surprised, and then puzzled and curious, as it became plain that his visitors' mission was not over. The theophany of Genesis 18 is unique in that it has dual but unrelated purposes.

'When the men got up to leave, they looked down towards Sodom, and Abraham walked along with them to see them on their way' (Genesis 18:16). Perfect love has driven all fear out of the heart and mind of Abraham.[1] He knows that his principal guest is none other than 'the Judge of all the earth', as he will later call him (verse 25). Yet he continues, unabashed, to play the perfect host, accompanying his visitors on their way. Besides, such polite attentiveness might also serve him to discover what was next on their agenda. There is plainly more to be revealed, if only he will be allowed to tag along.

Perhaps he stirs a little uneasily as he sees the men look down towards Sodom, and begin to move in that direction. He knows all about the wickedness of Sodom. He is also aware that there, along with his family, lives his nephew Lot. While they are walking silently along, he senses that the Lord is turning over in his mind some matter of great importance, and the Holy Spirit immediately reveals to us just what it is. 'Then the LORD said, "Shall I hide from Abraham what I am about to do? Abraham will surely become a great and powerful nation, and all nations on earth will be blessed through him. For I have chosen him, so that he will direct his children and his household after him to keep the way of the LORD by doing what is right and just, so that the LORD will bring about for Abraham what he has promised him"' (Genesis 18:17-19). This is the reasoning in the mind of the Second Person of the Trinity, the Lord Jesus Christ himself, as he muses about what he is going to do and whether or not he should tell Abraham in advance.

An important decision

It is one of the most beautiful illustrations you will find anywhere in Scripture of the truth that, 'The Lord confides in those who fear him' (Psalm 25:14). Those who are closest to the Lord seem to have fewer problems about discerning the Lord's will because he loves to share his secrets with them. They are also those who learn to recognise the Lord's finger-prints in the mundane affairs of everyday life.

Moreover, we have already noted that Abraham was renowned as 'God's friend'. Here he is now, walking with his God, the same Lord Jesus Christ who would one day say to his apostles, 'I have called you friends, for everything that I learned from my Father I have made known to you' (John 15:15). The Saviour communicates the very conversations spoken within the Godhead to his friends! What he did 4,000 years ago for Abraham, and what he did 2,000 years ago for his disciples, he still does for his friends today. Are we the friends of the Saviour? On that same occasion in the upper room Jesus gave this definition: 'You are my friends if you do what I command' (John 15:14). Then, just as with Abraham here in Genesis 18, the Saviour emphasises that he personally selects his friends for a purpose. 'You did not choose me, but I chose you and appointed you to go and bear fruit — fruit that will last' (John 15:16). The Lord confides in all his friends, so that they might play their part in building his kingdom.

There is no reason why God should share anything with us. In fact, the main argument in these verses the Saviour advances in favour of taking Abraham into his confidence seems to be, 'Because I have given him so much grace, I ought to give him more.' We should be thankful that divine logic is superior to ours!

The Lord also reflects, in verse 19, on the fact that Abraham will soon be bearing a grave responsibility. If he is going to direct his children in the way of the Lord, then he needs to *understand* the way of the Lord. The Saviour surely reasons that to encourage Abraham to trust him, it would be helpful to show that he trusts Abraham.

A step of great daring

So the decision having been made, the little party comes to a stop, and the Lord speaks out loud for the first time since leaving Abraham's encampment at Mamre. 'The outcry against Sodom and Gomorrah is so great and their sin is so grievous that I will go down and see if what they have done is as bad as the outcry that has reached me. If not, I will know' (Genesis 18:20-21). Just as Abel's blood cried out from the ground for vengeance,[2] so did the wickedness of Sodom.

The Lord did not, of course, need to go down to that evil city and walk its streets or peer through its windows in order to know the truth of the matter. But he wanted Abraham to see that God's judgements are always fair and the result of a minute and painstaking investigation of all the facts. That will be one of the primary purposes of the Day of Judgement itself. The idea of a great tribunal where the whole truth is finally exposed is so that the whole universe will acknowledge not only that justice has been done, but that justice has been *seen* to be done. Every creature will be forced to admit that every decision of God has been utterly right.

Immediately Abraham hears the Lord speak these words, all his growing fears are confirmed and he is filled with a sudden and a deep consternation. The Lord has not exactly said he will destroy Sodom but Abraham knows only too well what he will find when he arrives there and the implications are inescapable. Not only do his own family live in Sodom, but also many others he knows, some of whom, you may remember, he had rescued from invading armies back in chapter 14. Indeed, on that occasion, the king of Sodom himself had come out and personally thanked Abraham for all he had done. He *knew* the people there; he could picture their faces. Though he detested their wickedness with a holy repugnance, nonetheless he did not feel he could stand idly by and watch their destruction.

So he takes a step of infinite daring. It is always important in the narrative passages of the Bible to try to picture in your mind what is happening . Not only do historical events become more vivid and more easily lodged in the memory, often significant details come to the fore that would otherwise easily be passed over. A good example of this occurs in the very next verse. 'The men turned away and went towards Sodom, but Abraham remained standing before the LORD' (Genesis 18:22). Christ's two angelic companions turn away from Abraham after this pause in order to continue their solemn reconnaissance mission, but Abraham stands directly in the Lord's path and will not let him pass. The Lord has declared that he, personally, wishes to survey Sodom, not merely send his agents. I assume, therefore, that he made as if to walk on with them but Abraham cuts in front of him and bars his progress.

Not only does he do that, but we are told in verse 23, 'Then Abraham approached him.' They were presumably standing close to each other to start with, so what does it mean that he 'approached' him?' Well Abraham comes right up to the Lord, as close as he can, toe to toe. There is something defiant, almost aggressive, in this action. Interestingly, the word used here, both in the original Hebrew and in the Greek translation widely read in New Testament times, is the same as that used elsewhere to describe the approach of hearts and minds to God in worship. 'Let us then approach the throne of grace with confidence' (Hebrews 4:16). Confidence? Do you think Abraham was confident as he boldly approached the Lord God there on the road to Sodom? I imagine he was filled with tremendous trepidation and that his heart was pounding at his own temerity. Part of him was probably saying, 'What on earth are you doing, you fool? Step back! Get out of the way! This has got nothing to do with you. You've had a good time with the Lord so far. Don't ruin it now! Those Sodomites deserve everything that's coming to them. And that probably goes for Lot, too, if you'd only face the facts of the matter. Don't get involved! Step aside, while you can!'

The prayer of Abraham

But this godly man was not prepared to listen to any such advice, for we read, 'Abraham approached him and said . . .' There then follows not only the first intercessory prayer of the Bible, but perhaps the finest example of them all. Being the first, it is given in detail and should be regarded as a prototype and pattern for believers to follow. It is a particularly desperate case he is pleading, and he knows it. That in itself should be a great encouragement to us. It prevents us from feeling, 'Well, I would like to pray for this but the situation is really so bad, how can I?'

Now no situation could be as bad as the situation in Sodom. No individual for whose conversion you might pray is as evil as some of those men for whom Abraham is about to pray. He knows that he must do so, and it is particularly glorious because so utterly selfless. There is no self-interest in this prayer at all. The outcome will not affect him directly. He is praying for those who will not pray for themselves. His intercession is fervent, reverent, persistent and definite. It is everything that should characterise a Christian's prayer for the spiritually lost. It is, of course, exactly what the Lord intended to draw forth when he shared his secret with his friend.

I dearly hope that when we study a prayer like this our hearts are greatly stirred and we want to follow Abraham's example. If only, as believers, we would look on the world around us with compassion rather than simply condemnation! If only we had the heart of Abraham! Whatever truths the Lord shares with us from his Word should be turned to either praise or petition. We should do this automatically. The reading of Scripture and prayer always belong together.

Why is it that we do not pray like this, when we know that all around us men and women are already under condemnation? Is it that, unlike Abraham, we are not utterly convinced of the terror and the awesomeness of God's holy judgement? Let us remind ourselves of this magnificent act of intercession. 'Then Abraham approached him and said: "Will you sweep away the righteous with the wicked? What if there are fifty righteous people in the city? Will you really sweep it away and not spare the place for the sake of the fifty righteous people in it? Far be it from you to do such a thing — to kill the righteous with the wicked, treating the righteous and the wicked alike. Far be it from you! Will not the Judge of all the earth do right?"

'The Lord said, "If I find fifty righteous people in the city of Sodom, I will spare the whole place for their sake." Then Abraham spoke up again: "Now that I have been so bold as to speak to the Lord, though I am nothing but dust and ashes, what if the number of the righteous is five less than fifty? Will you destroy the whole city because of five people?" "If I find forty-five there," he said, "I will not destroy it."

'Once again he spoke to him, "What if only forty are found there?" He said, "For the sake of forty, I will not do it." Then he said, "May the Lord not be angry, but let me speak. What if only thirty can be found there?" He said, I will not do it if I find thirty there."

'Abraham said, "Now that I have been so bold as to speak to the Lord, what if only twenty can be found there?" He said, "For the sake of twenty, I will not destroy it." Then he said, "May the Lord not be angry, but let me speak just once more. What if only ten can be found there?" He answered, "For the sake of ten, I will not destroy it"' (Genesis 18:23-32).

How beautifully the tension is built up, and yet it is all so desperately simple. Notice he is not merely praying that the 'righteous people' in Sodom should be saved, be there fifty or only ten of them. He is praying that the *whole city* should be saved for the sake of the righteous who are in it. So it is a very broad and generous prayer, worthy of any New Testament saint.

In order to pray such a prayer such as this, Abraham reveals that he has grasped three vital truths which many Christians today either do not fully understand or seem not quite to believe. Grasping these truths will, I believe, help us to begin to argue in prayer for our unsaved neighbours and the world at large in a way that is new, exciting, and, most important of all, thoroughly biblically rooted. Abraham's prayer is based on a premise, a presumption and a principle.

A premise

The major premise which lies behind this whole prayer is the righteousness of God. You may think we can take this for granted but in my view it requires highlighting. I am convinced that a proper understanding of the righteousness of God would change the very nature of our prayer and transform our whole approach.

There are two questions in this eighteenth chapter of Genesis that are extremely frequently quoted. We have previously considered the first, 'Is anything too hard for the Lord?' We often cite that little phrase, which appears in verse 14. The second question is posed by Abraham during his prayer in verse 25, 'Will not the Judge of all the earth do right?'

That is the major premise on which he builds his whole case — the righteousness of God. He is absolutely certain that God will act with perfect rectitude. Never in this prayer does Abraham forget his own position or question God's will. Nor does he try to suggest that the inhabitants of Sodom deserve anything less than total destruction. He does not try to minimise their guilt or the evil they have performed. He knew they were inexcusable. Of all the cities of Canaan, only the cities of the plain, which included Sodom and Gomorrah, had tasted God's mercy in miraculous deliverance from invasion. Only they had heard the voice of Melchizedek. Above all, Sodom itself had been privileged with the testimony of Lot, who, for all his failings, was still a righteous man.[3] All of these mercies they had despised. Their sin was grossly aggravated by their refusal to heed in any way these gracious providences. Abraham was under no illusions as he came to prayer. He pleads that the cup of judgement might pass from them, and yet we sense it is always, 'Not my will, but yours be done' (Luke 22:42).

His dependence on God's righteousness is shown in the calm assurance of his delivery. There is no panic in this prayer, as there often is when believers seem to be doubting God's justice. You may be as bold and direct and even as confrontational in prayer as Abraham is here, but never let it appear that you do not trust the Lord's judgement. There is a great deal of difference between passion and panic. We rest upon the solid assurance that the Judge of all the earth shall always do right, even when we would judge differently. What arrogance we so often display when we pit our puny, ignorant and sinful minds against the mind of God. '"For my thoughts are not your thoughts, neither are your ways my ways," declares the LORD. "As the heavens are higher than the earth, so are my ways higher than your ways and my thoughts than your thoughts"' (Isaiah 55:8-9).

There is authority and power in calm assurance. A crowd of people are on the verge of panic. One person lifts up their voice with calm assurance and everyone becomes quiet, attentive, expectant, hopeful.

That is the effect of a prayer which is squarely based on the righteousness of God, even when offered in the most desperate of circumstances. Its effect upon God himself may be incalculable.

Abraham's faith in the righteousness of God is also shown in the fine judgement that he exercised while praying, in knowing when to stop. This is one of the most difficult and delicate areas in the Christian life and it is rarely discussed. When do we know that it is right to stop praying for someone or something? Many Christians have never had to face this particular problem because, if answers to prayer do not come swiftly, they soon give up praying, not as the result of any conscious decision, but by default. Most of us, perhaps, stop praying for things because we gradually forget or lose interest; we find more pressing and immediate items for prayer displace those that are older and now seem less urgent.

More conscientious pray-ers, however, know that regularly they must consciously make the decision to cease praying about certain matters and leave them with the Lord. It is then that a clear understanding of, and faith in, the righteousness of God prevents confusion and feelings of guilt. Such a solid conviction will even help us make such a decision.

Why did Abraham not go on to pray, 'What if only *five* righteous people can be found in Sodom?' Why did he not go the whole way and ask, 'Lord, what if only *one* righteous person can be found there?' Do you think that Abraham later suffered from self-recrimination, imagining that Sodom might have been saved if only he had been more persistent or exercised greater faith? I do not think so. Nowhere is Abraham charged with lack of faith. Rather, I believe he knew when to stop praying because he had such a firm conviction that the Judge of all the earth would do right. He was able to sense when to carry on would somehow be a denial of that trust.

Unfortunately, the ten righteous people for whose sake God would have spared Sodom, were not to be found, and so the city was destroyed. No doubt, despite the gracious rescue of Lot and his daughters, Abraham was deeply saddened when he returned early the following morning to see dense smoke rising from the plain.[4] But he had no reason to blame himself and no thought of blaming God.

Basing our prayers on the premise of God's righteousness will console us in the midst of many perplexing providences, enabling us to pray and leave the outcome with the Lord. Ultimately, of course, this prayer reminds us that the salvation of the wicked is dependent not on the presence of the righteous ten, but on the presence of the Righteous One. When we plead the righteous life, death and resurrection of our Lord Jesus Christ, we shall see all of his people saved.

A presumption

Abraham's prayer is based securely on the premise of God's righteousness, but also on the presumption that there is an important distinction between accidents and punishment. Abraham knew that tragic accidents could take the lives of any, regardless of their spiritual standing or moral character. (He may even have been familiar with the ancient story of Job, whose 'comforters' tormented him precisely because they did not understand the distinction I am highlighting.) The reason why Abraham is sufficiently appalled to cry out to the Lord, 'Will you sweep away the righteous with the wicked?' (verse 23) is owing to the fact that the destruction of Sodom was clearly to be an act of judgement. Abraham was scandalised at the thought that a righteous God might punish indiscriminately. Accidents were indiscriminate, but not punishments.

In the summer of 1861, there was a whole series of terrible disasters, both natural and man-made, which filled the British newspapers. In response, the great C H Spurgeon was constrained to preach a sermon on Luke 13:1-5, where Jesus spoke about two tragic events that had recently occurred with similar loss of life. You will recall the lesson that the Saviour draws. Were those who died 'worse sinners' or 'more guilty' than anybody else? No, we all need to repent if we wish to escape final judgement, but in this life we must be careful not to derive unsafe and self-righteous conclusions from unusual and grievous providences.

Spurgeon firmly taught these conclusions in his famous sermon, which he aptly entitled *Accidents, not Punishments.* (David Livingstone thought it so good that he carried a copy of it in his box for many years all over Africa.) This prayer of Abraham is based on the presumption that there is an important difference between accidents and punishments. We need to be just as clear, though bearing in mind the lesson of Luke 13 that we are far more likely to be dealing with accidents rather than punishments.

Much of a believer's prayer life, both individually and corporately, is taken up responding to God's providential dealings with himself and others of his children. We need to develop a mature approach that does not assume every unfortunate happening is a mark of God's displeasure.

A principle

Abraham's prayer is based, thirdly, upon a very important principle: he understood that the righteous are 'the salt of the earth' (Matthew 5:13). Provided they have not lost their saltiness, that is, succumbed to a worldly lifestyle, Christians have a preservative effect upon the communities in which they live. You may well be aware of this truth, but when was the last time you based an intercessory prayer upon it? The whole of Abraham's prayer is founded on this principle.

Other images are used in the Gospels that reinforce the same point. In one of Jesus' parables, we learn that the weeds (representing the lost) are not immediately pulled for the sake of the wheat (representing the saved), which may otherwise be rooted up with them. Not many unbelievers can realise that their judgement is delayed, and therefore their gospel opportunity extended, simply because of the presence of Christians among them! But, of course, believers are intended to have an influence upon the world that is far more direct and positive than that.

In another parable, the Lord declared, 'The kingdom of heaven is like yeast that a woman took and mixed into a large amount of flour until it worked all through the dough' (Matthew 13:33). The same principle is being illustrated. Believers are left in the world for the world's salvation. The Lord takes 'no pleasure in the death of the wicked' (Ezekiel 33:11). Judgement is at least postponed because Christians are in the world, and God's desire is that through their words and example, many more might be saved.

Just think what that means. Every day, in countless ways, mercy triumphs over judgement, simply because of the presence of believers. God's righteousness in us extends beyond ourselves and mitigates the evils of the world. When nations have favoured believers, those nations have flourished as a direct result of this principle. Ultimately, when the salt is not sufficient, then the righteous are removed before judgement falls. That is what happened here at Sodom. It happened much earlier in the world of Noah's day. It is exactly what will happen when the end of this present world is imminent, when the days of distress will be shortened 'for the sake of the elect' (Matthew 24:22). Then God's people will be removed so that God's righteous judgement can fall.

A firm grasp of this principle will teach us not to despise the power of our testimony. We need to have a higher sense of the potential influence we can bear in the world. Only ten righteous people would have been enough to save Sodom. Reflect on that when you next bemoan the smallness of your local fellowship! Jude tells us that Sodom and Gomorrah 'serve as an example of those who suffer the punishment of eternal fire' (verse 7). God will not spare when the time is ripe. The final judgement is preparing even now.

We read that God would have destroyed the Israelites 'had not Moses, his chosen one, stood in the breach before him' (Psalm 106:23). Centuries later, we hear the Lord saying, 'I looked for a man among them who would build up the wall and stand before me in the gap on behalf of the land so I would not have to destroy it, but I found none' (Ezekiel 22:30). What a tragedy! It must not be repeated in our generation. How desperately today we need Christian men and women who will stand 'in the gap' and pray like Abraham and Moses of old.

Notes

1 1 John 4:18.

2 Genesis 4:10.

3 2 Peter 2:7.

4 Genesis 19:27-28.

Homeward bound

Genesis 26

After the dreadful judgement of Sodom and the other cities of the plain, Abraham and his people left Mamre, near Hebron, and moved south, eventually settling at Beersheba, on the edge of the Negev desert. There Abraham made a treaty with Abimelech, the king of the colony of Philistines, whose influence stretched at that time from Beersheba to the coast.

Beersheba

The very name *Beersheba* was chosen by Abraham to commemorate this agreement, which was sufficient to convince him that here was the place to settle. 'Abraham planted a tamarisk tree in Beersheba, and there he called upon the name of the LORD, the Eternal God. And Abraham stayed in the land of the Philistines for a long time' (Genesis 21:33, 34). In fact, he probably lived mostly in Beersheba until his death. In all likelihood it was there that Isaac, the child of promise, was finally born amidst much rejoicing.

It was to Beersheba that both father and son returned after the terrible test on Mount Moriah.[1] Though this was obviously one of the most significant episodes in both their lives, it lies outside the scope of this book. It is likely that both heard the voice of the Angel of the Lord but there was no *appearance* of the Son of God and therefore no theophany according to our strict definition. We are twice distinctly told that the Lord called 'from heaven'.

Sarah managed to return to her beloved Hebron to die and there Abraham bought a field from the Hittites for a burial site. Isaac was thirty-seven years old when he lost his mother,[2] with whom he had evidently been particularly close. He was a quiet and a sensitive young man and her death affected him very greatly. His temperament could not easily bear the knowledge that he was to be the man through whom God was to work out his loving purposes for all humanity. Just imagine how it must have felt to have that burden upon him, to realise that, humanly speaking the whole future redemption of the human race depended upon him!

Isaac moves out

Following Sarah's death, Isaac was never the same. He grew restless and moved out of the family home, trailing further south to live at Beer Lahai Roi,[3] the well in the desert, you may remember, where the Lord God had appeared to Hagar. Somehow, he breathed more easily in the clear desert air, relishing the isolation and freedom of the wilderness. Perhaps, in his grief and his loneliness, he identified with his mother's former maidservant, Hagar. Perhaps he felt somewhat estranged, just as she had. Maybe he hoped in going to Beer Lahai Roi that there the Lord would appear to *him*, and become *real* to him, as he so clearly was to his father. After all, if he truly was the Son of promise, should he not experience a theophany at least once in his life? He could certainly do with some divine confirmation. There seemed to be such a distance between himself and the Lord . . .

Maybe Satan had sown some doubts into his mind. Perhaps all the stories about the Lord's appearing were simply that, stories. The mind could play strange tricks. The years pass swiftly in Beer Lahai Roi but, during that time, nothing of any spiritual significance occurs. I am sure there are many believers who can identify with Isaac in his loneliness, fear and occasional jealousy.

It was on a visit back to his father Abraham in Beersheba that, by divine coincidence, he arrives at the same time as his future wife Rebekah. She was Isaac's second cousin and had been sought and found amongst the godfearing remnant of the family still living in far off Haran. At last he had found a soul-mate, and, significantly, we read, 'Isaac brought her into the tent of his mother Sarah, and he married Rebekah. So she became his wife, and he loved her; and Isaac was comforted after his mother's death' (Genesis 24:67). It takes a long time to get over the death of a mother, especially when a son is as sensitive a soul as Isaac. It was three years before he was 'comforted'.[4]

All the patriarchs had failings, and Isaac was no exception, as we shall see. Let it nonetheless be remembered that he was unique among them in that he was faithful to one wife all his life long, according to God's original design. Here was a true love match that was never tarnished or compromised.

The newly-weds return to Beer Lahai Roi, where spiritually Isaac continues to languish. The main reason for this is not hard to find. He is so unsure about his destiny, so uncomfortable with the burden of expectation upon him, that when they discover Rebekah is unable to conceive, he is far from distraught. For twenty years Isaac fails to accept the spiritual challenge God has set him in this. Finally, he submits to his divine calling, prays to the Lord for a child, and is promptly rewarded with twins![5] How patient God is with us and how gracious when at last we bend our stubborn wills to his.

The sad consequences of resentment

Another indication of Isaac's fragile spiritual state at the time can be seen in the fact that it is *Rebekah alone* who continues to enquire of the Lord regarding the significance of her pregnancy and it is to *Rebekah alone* that the Lord replies. He imparts some truly momentous information to her concerning her children's future, not least that 'the older will serve the younger' (Genesis 25:23). Everything she is told she doubtless relates to her husband.

Now just imagine how Isaac feels. God has never spoken to him directly; even on Mount Moriah it was his father who was addressed. Any thoughts he might have entertained of actually being granted a theophany have faded long ago. He feels excluded. He tries to escape the pain of this by hiding in a desert region, away from all social contact. He longs for communion with God but is afraid of what it might entail. His fear of spiritual commitment even causes him to distance himself from his godly wife. He dare not let her help him. When finally brought to pray about Rebekah's barrenness, she immediately conceives, just as he had feared! Now, the Lord is bypassing him once again — speaking to his wife instead of him. God had spoken to his father, not his mother! What did the Lord have against him? All his old neuroses once again hold him in their grip.

Have you ever felt like this? 'Why is it God always seems to speak to other people? He never seems to speak to me. I always seem to hear second-hand.' If you are ever tempted to think similar thoughts, you will readily identify with this sensitive and complex character, Isaac, and you will be intrigued to discover how God deals with him.

It was probably at this early stage that Isaac decided that he would only believe and act on what the Lord told him directly. So, for example, he would continue to assume the spiritual line would pass through the first-born unless he heard personally from God to the contrary! There are many modern-day Isaacs in our congregations who say, 'I do not care what the Bible says. Unless the Lord confirms it to *me*, I shall not believe it, I shall not do it.' We can be very proud and stubborn on spiritual things when we are far from the Lord.

Sadly, for another fifteen years, all through his sons' vital, formative years, Isaac continued to live not only physically but also spiritually in the wilderness. Then, when the boys were in their teens, the Lord took a double initiative. First, he took his faithful old 'friend', Abraham to be with himself, at the age of 175. He was buried alongside his dear wife Sarah, back in Hebron.

Secondly, we read in Genesis 25:11, 'After Abraham's death, God blessed his son Isaac, who then lived near Beer-Lahai-Roi.' Isaac was now the head of the chosen family, whether he liked it or not. 'Abraham left everything he owned to Isaac' (Genesis 25:5). He could no longer shirk all family involvement and responsibility, and so the Lord decides to take Isaac in hand. He is now seventy-five years old. His utter unpreparedness for spiritual leadership is perfectly conveyed by the blatant favouritism he shows towards his first-born Esau, despite the infinitely greater spiritual tastes of Jacob, the son of God's choice.[6] The time for Isaac's spiritual recovery to begin is now or never. Something has to be done, and that something is related in Genesis 26.

A famine in the land

Genesis 26 is the only chapter in the Book in which Isaac is indisputably the chief character. This is surprising when you consider that Abraham, Jacob and Joseph each feature prominently in about twelve chapters apiece. I do not mention this to minimise the importance of Isaac but rather to maximise the significance of this much neglected chapter. The reason for its neglect is its lack of any single, big, dramatic incident, but its genius lies elsewhere. This chapter unfolds a wonderful story of spiritual restoration over a period of years. Nothing happens suddenly. It relates the way in which the Lord gradually restores a perplexed and wayward disciple to the place of blessing. It is the story of how Isaac is brought home. Though spanning a comparatively short episode in the life of the longest-lived of all the patriarchs,[7] the significance of this period is indicated by two theophanies, one at the beginning and the other at the end. They were to be the only occasions on which the Lord appeared to the son of Abraham.

The Lord's scheme for blessing and restoring Isaac does not start in the way that you or I would imagine. 'Now there was a famine in the land — beside the earlier famine of Abraham's time — and Isaac went to Abimelech, king of the Philistines in Gerar' (Genesis 26:1), with the apparent intention of continuing on to Egypt. It is surely no coincidence that the three foundational patriarchs, Abraham, Isaac and Jacob, who are so constantly named together in the Word of God, each had to face a major famine, and each instinctively turned to the grain house of the whole region, Egypt, to provide a solution.

The outcome was different in every case but Abraham, Isaac and Jacob were all similarly tested. These famines provided an ideal way for the Lord to try the faith and refine the graces of his chosen ones, and so the beginning of the chapter indicates a stirring of the Lord on Isaac's behalf.

As in the Parable of the Lost Son,[8] a famine could well be used by God to bring about a firmer grasp of spiritual reality and a truer sense of spiritual priority. The Lord continues to send 'famines' into the lives of his people. We may actually experience a genuine shortage of material necessities, but more often for us it is a spiritual famine. It seems a paradoxical thing to do. You are away from the Lord and he sends you a spiritual famine, so that you are drier and more malnourished than ever.

The idea is that, as with the Lost Son, we shall be brought back to our senses and out of sheer desperation, begin to ask the questions that really matter. But if there is a spiritual famine in your life at the moment, you are certainly not going to be relieved of it by going down to whatever equivalent you may find to the granaries of Egypt. The world may obliterate a sense of spiritual concern but it cannot satisfy it. The Lord always provides a way of escape if we are prepared to listen out for and obey his word.

It is at this point that Isaac is stopped in his tracks. Arriving in the capital city of this coastal colony of the Philistines, the Lord not only speaks to him but grants him the theophany he gave up dreaming about decades before.

A divine challenge

'The LORD appeared to Isaac and said, "Do not go down to Egypt; live in the land where I tell you to live. Stay in this land for a while, and I will be with you and will bless you. For to you and your descendants I will give all these lands and will confirm the oath I swore to your father Abraham. I will make your descendants as numerous as the stars in the sky and will give them all these lands, and through your offspring all nations on earth will be blessed, because Abraham obeyed me and kept my requirements, my commands, my decrees and my laws"' (Genesis 26:2-5).

We do not need to examine these words; they should now be familiar to us. They are a repetition of the glorious covenant promises made to Abraham. He is saying to Isaac, 'There! You did not think I was going to speak to you, let alone appear to you! Of course you are the child of promise! Your faith and obedience have not been of the same order as your father's, but for his sake I will bless you. And the One who will bring hope to the world will trace his human descent through you.'

It was all in God's good time. It is no use asking why the Lord waited until Isaac was well into his seventies before intervening in this way. He has his own plans and purposes and all the time in the world in which to bring them to pass. We are so impatient, so unlike God. How important it is to learn to take King David's advice: 'I am still confident of this: I will see the goodness of the LORD in the land of the living. Wait for the LORD; be strong and take heart and wait for the LORD' (Psalm 27:13-

14). No matter how it may sometimes appear, our God is not indifferent, nor does he play games with our lives.

Now although the Lord allowed Abraham at this stage in the 'famine test' to go on down into Egypt, he does not do so with Isaac. The simplest explanation is that the Lord tailor-makes all our circumstances and all our situations individually. Just because a friend was guided in a certain direction in similar circumstances to your own is no guarantee that you are meant to follow. Such carelessness has led to many terrible mistakes. We need to learn from the many similar situations presented in Scripture, where history seems to repeat itself. Reading through Genesis, for example, several scenarios recur in successive generations but there are always differences to be observed.

All this helps us to realise that while we are to learn from history, we are not slavishly to follow it. God deals with each one of his children on a personal basis and your experience will never be identical to that of anybody else. If he does not bless us as he blesses others, it does not necessarily mean we are out of his favour. Let us rather be encouraged that he has an individual plan for each one of us.

For Isaac to go down to Egypt under famine conditions was the normal and obvious course of action to take. It was the natural solution to the difficulty. What Isaac did not know was that God was going to produce a supernatural solution that he could not foresee. The grass not only *looked* greener in Egypt; it *was* greener! Yet the Lord commanded, 'Stay in this land for a while, and I will be with you and will bless you.' God says to him, 'Trust me and you will see how things change.'

Many believers have missed God's best for them because they have followed an 'obvious' course of action against the Lord's wishes. Beware of 'obvious' courses of action without reference to the Lord. It is foolish, in any case, to run away from a famine situation without learning anything from it. If the Lord has put you there, it is in order to bless. Get a bigger view of the providence of God! It is not always his intention that we escape from 'bad' situations. We often learn most in adversity. 'When you *pass through* the waters, I will be with you; and when you *pass through* the rivers, they will not sweep over you. When you *walk through* the fire, you will not be burned; the flames will not set you ablaze. For I am the LORD, your God, the Holy One of Israel, your Saviour' (Isaiah 43:2-3).

What blessings we would miss if we always sought to escape painful and fraught circumstances instead of going 'through' them with the Lord! Maybe the grass looks greener somewhere else to you at the moment. Maybe the grass *is* greener there. But it does not necessarily mean that God wants you to go!

Writing to believers undergoing severe persecution, the apostle Peter wrote, 'In this you greatly rejoice, though now for a little while you may have had to suffer grief in all kinds of trials. These have come so that your faith — of greater worth than gold, which perishes even though refined by fire — may be proved genuine and may result in praise, glory and honour when Jesus Christ is revealed' (1 Peter 1:6-7).

'So Isaac stayed in Gerar' (Genesis 26:6), and in so doing became the only patriarch never to leave the Promised Land.

Statement of faith

Despite the appearance of the Son of God to Isaac, it took faith to believe the promise, 'I will be with you' (verse 3), when up until that time the Lord had seemed very distant from him for many years. And I am afraid that although he stayed in the land, he did not begin this new phase of his life very well. Through fear he tried the trick he had learnt from his father of passing off his wife as his sister. But Isaac found that Abimelech the king had a far higher moral code than he ever suspected.[9]

It is always lack of faith that imagines the Lord would place us undefended in positions of moral danger. He will never do that. We may find ourselves in very trying circumstances, but there is always a God-honouring path that can be followed.[10] The Lord will certainly never require us to lie and cheat in order to fulfil his commands. Isaac should have known that, but at least he learned a lesson out of it and in his shame, made no attempt to excuse his sin.

That he could fall so swiftly after receiving such a revelation shocked Isaac into a determined demonstration of faith. He decided to plant some crops (verse 12). This was a deliberate act of faith for a number of reasons. First, 'There was a famine in the land' (verse 1). Secondly, he had not intended to stay there in Gerar. It was merely to have been a stopping-off place on the way to the safe haven afforded in the lands watered by the dependable River Nile.

Thirdly, Isaac was no arable farmer. He was a cattle man. He had never sown seed before. (In fact, it is the first reference to the planting of crops in the Bible.) No doubt many of the local farmers shook their heads in pitying disbelief at this stranger's foolhardiness, but Isaac felt this was the best way of showing the Lord that he really meant business and was resolved to stay. Isaac declares his commitment to the land and a reliance on God's promises concerning it in much the same way as did Jeremiah when, many centuries later, despite the Babylonian invasion, he bought a field at Anathoth.[11] Isaac literally put down roots and cast himself upon the providence of God.

Sometimes, all the Lord wants from us is an indication of commitment to our situation. In this case, he really honours the exercise of faith by a backslidden child of his who has only known self-pity in recent years. It must have thrilled God's heart to see this man who was not used to acting and operating in faith suddenly trusting him in a remarkable manner.

'Isaac planted crops in that land and the same year reaped a hundredfold, because the LORD blessed him. The man became rich, and his wealth continued to grow until he became very wealthy' (Genesis 26:12-13). Now that was some response! Isaac had simply come to the point of saying, 'All right Lord, I give in. Let's do it your way. I have seen I have no strength of my own. I am going to stop fighting. I have been pretty miserable battling against you, anyway. I have wanted everything to revolve around me and to be done as I saw fit. I really thought you were against me and were letting things get out of hand. Forgive me! I want to show you that, come what may, it is now my set purpose to trust you.'

Would the Lord not be delighted to hear *any* of his rebellious children expressing such a repentant spirit? Of course he would! And such is his grace that they would soon find, in return, 'a good measure, pressed down, shaken together and running over' being poured into their lap

(Luke 6:38). The Lord blesses Isaac immeasurably more than he could ever have asked or imagined,[12] to such an extent that the people around, all those unbelieving Philistines, are staggered and filled with envy.

It has been said that times of abundance reveal believers' vices, while times of scarcity reveal their virtues. That is why God sends famine to backslidden believers — not to punish, but to restore. When we sow to the Spirit in times of spiritual famine we may well reap a harvest of righteousness that can be both immense and immediate. 'Isaac planted crops in that land and the same year reaped a hundredfold.' It is all of grace.

The persecution of Isaac

Unfortunately, that did not mean that Isaac's troubles were over. Far from it! 'He had so many flocks and herds and servants that the Philistines envied him. So all the wells that his father's servants had dug in the time of his father Abraham, the Philistines stopped up, filling them with earth. Then Abimelech said to Isaac, "Move away from us; you have become too powerful for us"' (Genesis 26:14-16). God's blessing often leads to envy on the part of the people of the world. Envy leads to fear. Fear leads to persecution. 'In fact,' Paul confided to Timothy, 'everyone who wants to live a godly life in Christ Jesus will be persecuted' (2 Timothy 3:12). It is inevitable.

We cannot love the Lord and the world at the same time, and once we show we love the Lord, the world will soon show it does not love us. But in response to these trials, the spiritual qualities which had lain dormant in Isaac for so many years are abruptly and gloriously reawakened. The quiet submission to God's will that had been so astonishingly impressive in the young man who permitted himself to be bound and placed on an altar on Mount Moriah, was suddenly evident again.

The Philistines filled in all Abraham's wells out of sheer spite. They had no right to do that; a man's wells were his own property. It was also an act of stupidity. Abimelech was right when he said, 'You have become too powerful for us.' Isaac undoubtedly had the muscle by now to have defended his territory or exacted retribution. He could have held on grimly to the land he was farming and no one could have prevented it. Yet, he does not do that. He who was a type of Christ on Mount Moriah becomes a type of Christ again. 'When they hurled their insults at him, he did not retaliate; when he suffered, he made no threats. Instead, he entrusted himself to him who judges justly' (1 Peter 2:23).

'So Isaac moved away from there and encamped in the Valley of Gerar and settled there. Isaac reopened the wells that had been dug in the time of his father Abraham, which the Philistines had stopped up after Abraham died, and he gave them the same names his father had given them. Isaac's servants dug in the valley and discovered a well of fresh water there. But the herdsmen of Gerar quarrelled with Isaac's herdsmen and said, "The water is ours!" So he named the well Esek ['dispute'], because they disputed with him. Then they dug another well, but they quarrelled over that one also; so he named it Sitnah ['opposition']. He moved on from there and dug another well, and no one quarrelled over it. He named it Rehoboth ['room'], saying, "Now the LORD has given us room and we will flourish in the land"' (Genesis 26:17-22).

He keeps giving ground. The Philistines dispute a well and he moves back again, further up the Valley of Gerar. But this is not just passive non-resistance on the part of Isaac. No, all the time he is digging out the earth from his father's old wells as well as digging new ones of his own. Here is active perseverance, as he fights desperately to provide the vital water for his people, herds and flocks.

The commentators have always loved to spiritualise these verses. In 1959, Martyn Lloyd-Jones preached a series of six sermons on verses 17 and 18, listing all the hindrances that need to be cleared away before the living waters of revival can flow again in the church.[13] These are glorious, stirring messages that continue to speak powerfully to those who read them, but I am not sure they are legitimate exposition of the text!

One thing is clear. Isaac would not have bothered to dig a new well whenever it was possible to undertake the far simpler and more certain task of reopening an old one. This illustrates a helpful principle. To change the metaphor, Christians today love to reinvent the wheel, whereas a little knowledge of how wheels were made by our spiritual forefathers and of the old paths on which they ran so well could result in far greater spiritual progress.

Having said that, even digging where we know our fathers have been successful requires effort, and, as here, is still no guarantee that we shall be permitted to drink the water. There are no short cuts or easy options when it comes to growing in grace and holiness.

The homecoming

The ending of the story of Genesis 26 is particularly poignant and highly instructive. Just when Isaac had succeeded in proving his rekindled trust in the Lord, just when he thought he had received the gracious reward of 'room' to 'flourish' and just when he had begun to think, 'This is where the Lord finally wants me to be', he discovers something that changes everything and makes sense of it all.

I do not suppose Isaac had thought about it, but as he was being pushed further and further south-east, up the Gerar valley, he suddenly realises that he is close to his old home of Beersheba. Maybe, one day, he was struck by the strange familiarity of the landscape and memories of his boyhood started flooding back. 'Why, it must be Beersheba over that hill. Maybe just for old times sake I will pay a little visit. They really were happy days, now I think of it, all those many years ago.'

We have to read between the lines because the Scripture simply states, 'From there he went up to Beersheba' (Genesis 26:23), the 'well of the oath' his father had sworn together with an earlier Philistine king. From what follows, I imagine he goes alone, in a reflective mood. It had been his home for so long. He surely recalls many incidents, not least returning after that terrible time on Mount Moriah. But in those early years he had known much joy as he walked in fellowship with his Father in heaven, as well as his father on earth. Little did Isaac suspect what was about to happen.

'That night the LORD appeared to him and said, "I am the God of your father Abraham. Do not be afraid, for I am with you; I will bless you and will increase the number of your descendants for the sake of my servant Abraham"' (Genesis 26:24). Notice the change in the wording here from that of verse 3. In this second theophany it is no longer, 'I *will* be with you', but 'I *am* with you.' Can you imagine Isaac's feelings, receiving such a visitation on such a sacred spot?

And the message that screams out to me, and that I pass on to you, is simply this: 'Go back!' If you want fully and finally to recover the joy you once knew and the love you once felt for your Saviour, you may well find he will meet with you where once you left him. I am speaking spiritually, of course, in the way that we are to understand so much of Old Testament history. 'These things happened to them as examples [types] and were written down as warnings for us, on whom the fulfilment of the ages has come' (1 Corinthians 10:11).

In the light of this second appearance of the Son of God to him, Isaac begins to ask himself some serious questions. Why had he ever left Beersheba to go to Beer-Lahai-Roi, the place of *somebody else's* blessing? Why had he abandoned the very place where God had met with *him*?

If we have drifted gradually, imperceptibly away from true fellowship with the Lord, we need to ask ourselves similar questions. We need to seek him once again where in the past he met with us. I remember an old man who once came to me in tears with a tattered, yellowing sheet of paper torn from some ancient exercise book. It turned out to be the testimony of his conversion he had written down for reading at his baptism at the age of sixteen. He told me he had been turning out some old books and he had found it among them. Reading the words he had written over seventy years previously had driven him to his knees as he sought and found forgiveness and spiritual restoration after many years of spiritual apathy.

Perhaps you have a copy of the testimony of your 'first love' that you need to root out and ponder. What was that passage of Scripture that you always used to turn to whenever you grew spiritually cold? You have not turned to it for a long while. Remember the way you used to pray so fervently, the way the Lord seemed to bless so very often. Do you recall the wonderful sense of God's nearness that you enjoyed when you plucked up the courage to speak for your Saviour? You would do well to meditate on Psalm 77. Go back not only in your mind — there is no benefit in mere spiritual nostalgia — but in your practice. Go back to where the Lord blessed *you*.

For Isaac, Beersheba was the place where God had blessed him and where he would bless him again. How Isaac praised God that he had brought him home! 'Isaac built an altar there and called on the name of the LORD. There he pitched his tent, and there his servants dug a well' (Genesis 26:25). And that is where, not surprisingly, he and his family decided to stay, as the later chapters of Genesis reveal.

Confirmations

It is always good to know you are home. And to confirm it for Isaac, history repeated itself.[14] 'Meanwhile, Abimelech had come to him from Gerar, with Ahuzzath his personal adviser and Phicol the commander of his forces. Isaac asked them, "Why have you come to me, since you were hostile to me and sent me away?" They answered, "We saw clearly that the LORD was with you; so we said, 'There ought to be a sworn agreement between us'—between us and you. Let us make a treaty with you that you will do us no harm, just as we did not molest you but always treated you well and sent you away in peace. And now you are blessed by the LORD." Isaac then made a feast for them, and they ate and drank. Early the next morning the men swore an oath to each other. Then Isaac sent them on their way, and they left him in peace' (Genesis 26:26-31).

Isaac received the same form of confirmation that he was in the right place as his father Abraham had all those years before. 'When a man's ways are pleasing to the LORD, he makes even his enemies live at peace with him' (Proverbs 16:7).

'That day Isaac's servants came and told him about the well they had dug. They said, "We've found water!" He called it Shebah, and to this day the name of the town has been Beersheba' (Genesis 26:32-33). We are not to be overly influenced by 'favourable' providences when it comes to guidance but when we are finally in the place of God's choosing, numerous outward confirmations are not unusual. Through meekness, the Lord irresistibly drew Isaac home. We need that same spirit of meekness, so that we might be spiritually at home with the Lord, in the place of blessing, usefulness and joy.

Notes

1 The account is found in Genesis 22.
2 Compare Genesis 17:17 with 23:1.
3 Genesis 24:62.
4 See note 2 and compare Genesis 25:20.
5 Compare Genesis 25:20-21, 26.
6 Reflect on the well known incident recorded in Genesis 25:27-34.
7 Isaac lived to be 180 (Genesis 35:28-29).
8 Luke 15:11-32.
9 Genesis 26:7-11.
10 See 1 Corinthians 10:13.
11 Jeremiah 32:7-15.
12 Ephesians 3:20.
13 Reprinted in *Revival,* Marshall Pickering, 1986.
14 Compare Genesis 26:26-31 with 21:22-34. The names Abimelech and Phicol are probably titles. We need not believe that they were the same individuals in the two accounts.

Stairway to heaven

Genesis 28:10-22

Even though the theophany at Beersheba marked the culmination of his restoration, there remained one tragic blind spot in Isaac's spiritual recovery. He still would not accept the fact that God could have spoken to Rebekah and not him about the destiny of their twin sons. This issue continued to rankle over the decades and was still not resolved in his heart.

Most particularly, he would not accept that God had said the older would serve the younger.[1] So, for a very long time, he stubbornly favoured Esau, while Rebekah felt that she must compensate by lavishing her affection upon Jacob. It was, of course, even at the natural level, a recipe for disaster, and spiritually it created havoc. Isaac could not function properly as the head of his own household and much mischief and heartache resulted, as, in such circumstances, it always must.

Putting the record straight

God is sovereign and his will cannot be frustrated. He had decided to 'love' Jacob and to 'hate' Esau.[2] 'And we know that in all things God works for the good of those who love him, who have been called according to his purpose' (Romans 8:28). But just because God delights to bring good out of evil is no reason why we should do evil that good may come. Tragically, however, that is exactly what Rebekah and Jacob sought to do as they desperately schemed to bring about God's will by their own efforts.

Having said that, I do want us to be clear about the Bible's verdict on all the actors in the great drama that unfolds. Many Christians bring false preconceptions to the account of Esau bartering his birthright for a bowl of stew.[3] The same can be said when it comes to the outrageous scheme which occupies most of chapter 27 of Genesis, in which Jacob pretends to be his brother Esau in order to obtain the solemn covenantal blessing. This is one of the great narratives of the Old Testament, a tremendous story full of drama and tension. What is often forgotten is that, in both these incidents, the Bible lays the blame principally and squarely upon Esau and Isaac.

It is strange, and more than a little sad, that popular interpretations of these colourful events generally portray Esau as the honest, outgoing, likeable, trusting victim of his sly, pampered, unscrupulous, and rather nasty brother. That is the common view that has been passed down to us through the centuries and still appears in commentaries and school text books. One cannot help feeling that both conscious and unconscious anti-Semitism has moulded such a distorted view, casting Jacob, the immediate father of the tribes of Israel, in such a negative light.

It was Esau, not Jacob, who 'despised his birthright' (Genesis 25:34). He cared so little for his spiritual heritage that he married Hittite wives.[4] When, years later, it seemed to register that marrying Canaanite women was not exactly what was required, he tried to make up for it by marrying a daughter of Uncle Ishmael, who himself had been cast out from the godly line![5] He was simply pathetically out of tune with the will and way of the Lord. The writer to the Hebrews dismisses Esau with the single word 'godless' (Hebrews 12:16)..

None of this reflects too well on Isaac. What was Isaac doing allowing his son to marry pagans when, at the same age, his father Abraham had sent for a godly wife for him? And having allowed this to happen, how could Isaac possibly still believe that God would be prepared to preserve the Messianic line through such a man? It is almost beyond belief, and yet such is the power of blind prejudice, that, when Isaac believed himself to be near death, he was determined to bestow his patriarchal blessing on Esau as a final act of resentful defiance.

So when it comes to the great deception of chapter 27, we have to bear in mind that Rebekah and Jacob were desperate to prevent Isaac from taking this catastrophic and wilfully wicked course of action. The Bible does not explicitly condemn them for it, so we have reason to put the most favourable construction upon their actions. It is true that Rebekah and Jacob deceived and that Jacob also lied, but there were extenuating circumstances and their motives were honourable.

When, centuries later, the Hebrew midwives lied to Pharaoh in order to preserve the seed of Israel, we read that God was kind to them and blessed them.[6] There is no hint that the Lord felt any differently about Rebekah and Jacob here. Concerned as they were for God's glory, perhaps their greatest sin in his eyes was a lack of faith that he would work it out in his own way.

The humbling of Isaac

Whatever, it is Isaac who, after recovering from the shock of his deception, clearly finds true repentance. He is suddenly and dramatically humbled. When he discovers that Jacob has after all received the blessing, he sees the overruling hand of God in what has happened. He tells a distraught Esau, 'I blessed him, and indeed he will be blessed' (Genesis 27:33). Though overcome with the emotional impact of the moment, he surrenders this last area of rebellion with a spirit of holy resignation.

Far from gunning for his wife and his younger son, as might well have been expected, he now calmly takes Rebekah's advice and does what he should have done years before. He sends Jacob off, back to his father's house in Haran, to find a godly wife. In taking this decision, he acknowledges for the first time that the seed is to be preserved through Jacob and confirms it by pronouncing the covenantal, birthright blessing upon him once again. Only, this time, he does so even more fulsomely and without any nagging pricks of conscience. There is a true sense of release when we finally give up long-cherished but dubious beliefs and practices.

'So Isaac called for Jacob and blessed him and commanded him: "Do not marry a Canaanite woman. Go at once to Padan Aram, to the house of your mother's father Bethuel. Take a wife for yourself there, from among the daughters of Laban, your mother's brother. May God Almighty bless you and make you fruitful and increase your numbers until you become a community of peoples. May he give you and your descendants the blessing given to Abraham, so that you may take possession of the land where you now live as an alien, the land God gave to Abraham." Then Isaac sent Jacob on his way, and he went to Padan Aram, to Laban son of Bethuel the Aramean, the brother of Rebekah, who was the mother of Jacob and Esau' (Genesis 28:1-5).

Just as Isaac, for shame, had not shared with Rebekah his intention of actually passing on the blessing to Esau, so Rebekah still holds certain things to herself. Understandably, she is still a little uncertain of the extent to which the spiritual eyes of her husband Isaac have truly been opened. Can his thinking really have been changed so radically, so quickly and so apparently painlessly? The answer is, yes! The apostle Paul told the Roman believers, 'Do not conform any longer to the pattern of this world, but be transformed by the renewing of your mind' (Romans 12:2). The New Testament word for repentance means literally a change of mind. The Holy Spirit can and does 're-clothe us in our rightful mind'[7] in an instant.

Nevertheless, with so much at stake, we cannot blame Rebekah for being wary. She does not share with Isaac the main reason why she wanted Jacob to leave home now. She has discovered that Esau has sworn to kill his brother but fearing Isaac might not believe Esau to be capable of such a crime, she keeps it to herself. However genuine Isaac's change of heart might be, she is delighted that she scarcely needs to develop her ploy for getting Jacob away to safety.[8]

And so we read in Genesis 28:10, 'Jacob left Beersheba and set out for Haran.' He was seventy-seven years old, still in his prime, according to the slower ageing process of that day, but nearly twice as old as his father had been when he married. The difference represents the wasted years during which Isaac had kept waiting, vainly hoping that maybe Esau was to be the son of blessing.

How easy it is to let the years slip by in this way. All the evidence, from the gifts you possess to the advice of godly friends, points you in a certain direction in life. Yet you wait and wait and wait because you are convinced that the Lord will open up a different path. Are you wasting the precious time God has given you, waiting for something that will not happen? The cost can be immense in many ways, not just for you but for family and friends. There is often a narrow line between true faith and self-delusion. We all need to ask the Lord to keep us on the right side of it. I have little doubt that Isaac was full of remorse for his prolonged stubbornness in the matter and full of gratitude for the Lord's patient determination to overcome it.

Though their purpose was the same, the circumstances of Jacob's journey to Haran were very different from those of the party sent to find a wife for his father. Then, Abraham's servant had set out with a noble retinue and ten camels loaded with expensive gifts. Now, nearly a century later, Jacob sets out alone with no servants, no camels and no gifts. Years later, he was to recall that his only possession had been a staff.[9] When he left, Rebekah promised to send for her son as soon as his brother's fury subsided. We get the impression that she was thinking in terms of a few weeks or, at the most, months. It was not to be. Jacob was to be away for twenty years and, as far as we can gather, was never to see his mother again.

Thankfully, that knowledge did not further add to Jacob's misery as he set out on the long trek northwards, but the prospect was bleak enough. Here he was, a forlorn exile, fearful of what lay behind and before him. No doubt he was far from happy about his role in those recent, climactic events but he was comforted nonetheless by the reconciliation with his father, and dimly aware of his destiny. Two or three days' hard travelling brought him at nightfall into a weird valley, full of stones. Genesis 28:11 should begin, 'He chanced upon a certain place', but there was nothing 'hit and miss' about it from God's point of view. All our ways are planned with infinite care by an infinitely loving hand. Had Jacob but known it, this place was very near the site where once his grandfather Abraham had built an altar and called on the name of the Lord.[10]

A dream to remember

There, amidst the cries of the jackals and the night birds, he selected a stone for a headrest and settled down to sleep. He did not know that it was going to be one of the two most significant nights of his long life. Nor did he realise that where he slept would become for him the most precious spot on earth. The prophet Hosea puts it most succinctly. He simply says God 'found' Jacob at Bethel. And so he did.

'Jacob left Beersheba and set out for Haran. When he reached a certain place, he stopped for the night because the sun had set. Taking one of the stones there, he put it under his head and lay down to sleep. He had a dream in which he saw a stairway resting on the earth, with its top reaching to heaven, and the angels of God were ascending and descending on it. There above it stood the LORD, and he said: "I am the LORD, the God of your father Abraham and the God of Isaac. I will give you and your descendants the land on which you are lying. Your descendants will be like the dust of the earth, and you will spread out to the west and to the east, to the north and to the south. All peoples on earth will be blessed through you and your offspring. I am with you and will watch over you wherever you go, and I will bring you back to this land. I will not leave you until I have done what I have promised you"' (Genesis 28:10-15).

The fact that this first theophany granted to the patriarch Jacob was in the form of a dream is not essentially important. 'God spoke to our forefathers . . . in various ways' (Hebrews 1:1). This does not, of course, imply that anyone who dreams of seeing the Lord has received a divine revelation! Jacob may well have dreamt many times of seeing the Lord. He had thrilled to the stories about his grandfather and even his father doing exactly that. His spiritual longings had been aroused by his mother from an early age. Rebekah probably encouraged him to expect a theophany as proof of what the Lord had revealed to her about him before his birth. If he were truly a link in the chain of God's special blessing then surely he would receive the same miraculous confirmation as his forebears. It would be surprising if such fervent anticipation did not regularly take possession of his thoughts as he slept. But this was different! He had no difficulty in deciding that, of all his dreams, this one alone did not originate in his own head. Here was God revealing himself to a man. Here was true theophany!

Traditionally, we speak of 'Jacob's ladder' but I think our translation 'stairway' is a better one. The word appears only here in the Bible but is related to the word for 'siege ramps'. In Old Testament times these were great, wide, sloping mounds of earth that were piled up against city walls to provide access for the besieging army. This is more the picture we are to have in our minds. This 'stairway' was not only high, but sufficiently broad for perhaps countless angels to be seen both 'ascending and descending on it'.

In other words, it is a representation of the vast and complex intercourse that constantly proceeds between heaven and earth, totally unseen in the normal course of events by human eyes. The writer to the Hebrews tells us that there are, literally, 'myriads' of angels (12:22) and that their principal role is as 'ministering spirits sent to serve those who will inherit salvation' (1:14). It is glorious to contemplate these normally invisible, spiritual beings, whose task it is to protect, encourage and guide Christian believers.

A window on another world

Were God to open the right window for us, we would be able to see, as did Elisha's servant, 'the hills full of horses and chariots of fire all round' us (2 Kings 6:17), and all our natural fears would be allayed. Just because we do not see the reality is no denial of it.

You remember how Stephen in the New Testament, shortly before his martyrdom, 'looked up to heaven and saw the glory of God, and Jesus standing at the right hand of God. "Look," he said, "I see heaven open and the Son of Man standing at the right hand of God"' (Acts 7:55-56). No one else in that crowded meeting of the Sanhedrin saw anything extraordinary. It was just that God opened a window. It was as though, in the unpoetic parlance of cosmology, some 'wormhole' had been accessed into a parallel universe. It does not matter how you conceive the mechanism; it is beyond our understanding. There is a whole spiritual realm beyond our five natural senses that only the arrogance of so called 'scientific' materialism refuses to consider. No other living creature is capable of discovering all the truth of the cosmos. Why should human beings be the exception?

The point is that 'faith is being sure of what we hope for and certain of what we do not see' (Hebrews 11:1). How important it is for us to grasp that simply because we do not see the spiritual realm does not mean we are to think of it as being impossibly remote from our lives. Whenever a window is opened in the Scripture, it is for the great encouragement and strengthening of our faith. Jacob's stairway assures us that heaven is intensely interested in earth. There is continual spiritual communication between the two. There is no impassable gulf; indeed they are linked by a well-trodden path.

Mind-blowing promises

But Jacob's eyes do not dwell on the stairway, nor the angels upon it. His eyes are fixed on the One who stands at the top; poised, it would seem, to descend himself. The vision conveys the readiness, the eagerness, of the Son of God to come among the creatures made in his image. We may imagine him gazing longingly down the stairway.

Then the Saviour speaks, and all the covenant blessings that he had previously personally bestowed upon Abraham and Isaac, he now personally bestows upon Jacob. If Isaac's second attempt at pronouncing this blessing upon his son was more fulsome than his first, the promises that fell from the Saviour's own lips were the most profuse of all.

We may have been conditioned into thinking that Jacob was in a dreadful spiritual state at this time, but notice there is no word of rebuke for him. Quite the reverse. In fact, what is said makes the blessings that Isaac had received seem almost grudging. God truly did love Jacob! In any case, there is never any mention in heaven of the sins of those God has chosen. Whatever we may think of ourselves, or however others might condemn us, such is 'the grace of the Lord Jesus Christ, and the love of God, and the fellowship of the Holy Spirit' (2 Corinthians 13:14), that true Christians have nothing to fear. 'There is now no condemnation for those who are in Christ Jesus' (Romans 8:1).

Jacob receives not only the promise of the land and of a numerous progeny to possess it, he receives the messianic component as well: 'All peoples upon earth will be blessed through you and your offspring' (Gen. 28: 14). Jacob needed this great revelation to reassure him of all that his parents, especially his mother, had taught him. Here was his first personal contact with the Lord and we might well think of it as his spiritual conversion. Although he had always possessed spiritual instincts and longings, this close encounter with the Son of God revolutionised his life. Thank God when the truths our parents impressed upon us suddenly become real and vivid and personal to us. What a vital role believing parents have to play in sowing the seed in their children's lives.[11]

Of course, Jacob was now loaded with a great sense of responsibility. It is impossible to know how much he really understood. Did he have some faint realisation that the Lord at the head of the stairway would somehow take upon himself human flesh as one of his descendants? And, if so, could he have possibly understood why? Probably all he fully comprehended was that he had been singled out to shoulder an immense burden that may well have weighed him down rather than lifted him up.

All these mind-blowing promises seemed so remote to the lonely, frightened man who lay asleep in the dust of that rocky valley. How typically gracious of the Lord was it therefore to add words of personal comfort and reassurance. 'I am with you and will watch over you wherever you go, and I will bring you back to this land. I will not leave you until I have done what I have promised you' (verse 15). Has the Lord told *you* he is 'with you and will watch over you wherever you go'? He has if you are truly converted and are prepared to go where he leads you. Naturally, we should also always be praying Moses' prayer, 'If your Presence does not go with us, do not send us up from here' (Exodus 33:15).

Imagine the comfort that Jacob received from those final words: 'I will not leave you until I have done what I have promised you.' He says that to every faithful believer. Along with the apostle Paul, you may be absolutely confident 'that he who began a good work in you will carry it on to completion until the day of Christ Jesus' (Philippians 1:6).

Having mentioned that this theophany marks a radical turning point in Jacob's life, I want to consider his response to the Saviour's appearance as a model of conversion. It was when he saw Christ for himself that everything he had previously accepted on trust from his parents suddenly became real to him. Although we do not see Christ with our physical eyes still, spiritually speaking, 'There is life for a look at the Crucified One.'[12]

A mind transformed

The saving truth of the gospel must convince and transform the mind. 'When Jacob awoke from his sleep, he thought, "Surely the LORD is in this place, and I was not aware of it." He was afraid and said, "How awesome is this place! This is none other than the house of God; this is the gate of heaven"' (Genesis 28:16-17). This is not an untypical reaction in those who hear the Lord speaking to them for the first time. He never thought he could know God like this! He had always believed in the omnipresence of God, that he is everywhere. He did not share the Canaanite belief in merely local deities. It was not, as some liberal commentators suggest, that he was suddenly astonished that the God of his father could appear so far from home! What astonishes him is the vivid reality of this encounter, and the fact that it had been so unexpected.

I always like the title of C S Lewis's account of his conversion, *Surprised by Joy*. Jacob is 'surprised by joy' and all sorts of other emotions, but, as with Lewis, his mind is absolutely captivated and taken over. He awakes out of sleep in more senses than one. Wherever the soul feels the presence and power of the Lord, that soul becomes the house of God and the very gate of heaven. There is a sense of awe and holy fear, leaving no room any longer for a dispassionate, let alone flippant, discussion of the existence of God.

We should long to see today what Paul obviously expected to occur in Corinth if an unbeliever strayed under the sound of God's word. 'He will be convinced by all that he is a sinner and will be judged by all, and the secrets of his heart will be laid bare. So he will fall down and worship God, exclaiming, "God is really among you!"' (1 Corinthians 14:24-25). Believers also need a fresh view of Christ so that they may realise once again that God is in their situation, even though they were 'not aware of it'.

A heart opened and warmed

Conversion is seen not only in a transformed mind but also in a heart that is opened and warmed.[13] 'Early the next morning Jacob took the stone he had placed under his head and set it up as a pillar and poured oil on top of it. He called that place Bethel [house of God], though the city used to be called Luz' (Genesis 28:18-19). All cynicism is banished from him. He acts in a way he would only recently have condemned as pure sentiment. He sets up the stone he had used as a pillow to be a memorial of his life-changing experience. He pours oil upon it as an act of dedication — the first example in the Bible of a ritual that speaks of the anointing of the Holy Spirit.

Bethel was to become for Jacob a lifelong symbol of God's faithfulness. His heart is filled with love and gratitude in a way he had never previously thought possible. Every time he subsequently returned to this memorial, or even merely thought of it, his heart would leap for joy. How gracious it is of our God to continue to give us memorials. When we come to the Lord's Supper we handle the bread and we taste the wine. These are tangible reminders of something Christ has done for us infinitely greater than he did for Jacob at Bethel. How our hearts should be opened and warmed as we remember our Saviour's sacrifice on the cross.

A will redirected and established

A third vital component in any genuine conversion is a will redirected and established. 'Then Jacob made a vow, saying, "If God will be with me and will watch over me on this journey I am taking and will give me food to eat and clothes to wear so that I return safely to my father's house, then the LORD will be my God and this stone that I have set up as a pillar will be God's house, and of all that you give me I will give you a tenth' (Genesis 28:20-22).

It would be far better to read, '*Since* God will be with me . . .' rather than '*If* . . .' Jacob is not here striking a bargain with God! He is overcome with the mercy of the Lord towards him. 'Since God has promised all these things for me, he shall be Lord of my life.' Here is a pledge worthy of its place as the first vow in the Bible. A vow is an act of the will. Conversion affects the whole person — mind, heart and will. This wholehearted response speaks of the total consecration which should characterise any true conversion. All those who follow Christ should be prepared to say to him,

'Take my will, and make it thine;
It shall be no longer mine . . .'[14]

Jacob speaks of establishing worship at that sacred spot, and he will ultimately keep his vow in this regard, as we shall see. But that is another story.

The chapter closes with Jacob's announcement that he will begin to tithe to the Lord. Where does he get this notion from? He has no doubt heard the story of his grandfather Abraham's dealings with Melchizedek. But there was no law about it. There were only freewill offerings before the establishment of Old Testament Israel, as is the case once again, now that Old Testament Israel is no more. Jacob gives from a truly Christian motive, out of love and gratitude to the Lord for all he has done, is doing and will yet do for him. Tithing may well represent 'good practice' for the Christian believer, but only if it is as free of legalism as it was for Jacob.

'Of all that you give me I will give you a tenth' (verse 22). Those who, like Jacob, regard all they have as a gift from God rather than as essentially their own, find generous giving to the Lord's work rather less painful. It is not a question of how much I will give of my own substance to God but of how much of what God has given to me I can legitimately retain. The fundamental principles of Christian giving are all enshrined in three verses from one of Paul's letters. 'Remember this: Whoever sows sparingly will also reap sparingly, and whoever sows generously will also reap generously. Each man should give what he has decided in his heart to give, not reluctantly or under compulsion, for God loves a cheerful giver. And God is able to make all grace abound to you, so that in all things at all times, having all that you need, you will abound in every good work' (2 Corinthians 9:6-8).

The reality of Jacob's conversion may be best illustrated by contrasting Genesis 27:20 with Genesis 28:21. In the first verse he is in the act of deceiving his father when he says, 'The LORD *your* God gave me success.' In the second verse, as a result of the theophany at Bethel, he declares, 'The LORD will be *my* God.' Has your relationship to God completely changed because of an encounter with his Son?

Pontifex Maximus

Such a thought leads me to reflect on the light that Jesus himself shed on this theophany when he was gathering his first disciples. Nathanael declared his faith in Christ with the wonderful words, 'Rabbi, you are the Son of God; you are the King of Israel.' To which Jesus replied, 'I tell you the truth, you shall see heaven open, and the angels of God ascending and descending on the Son of Man' (John 1:49, 51). Christ not only stands at the top of the stairway, but he is, in a very real sense, the stairway itself. He is the only 'Way' for us to ascend to glory.[15] Looking to him, therefore, we see heaven opened not just once, but always.

In the fifth century AD, the Pope assumed the originally pagan title, *Pontifex Maximus,* which means, literally, *Greatest Bridgebuilder.* But no mere man can bridge the gulf between earth and heaven. One alone deserves the title. 'For there is one God and one mediator between God and men, the man Christ Jesus' (1 Timothy 2:5).

Notes

1 Genesis 25:23.

2 Malachi 1:2-3; Romans 9:13.

3 Genesis 25:29-34.

4 Genesis 26:34-35.

5 Genesis 28:6-9.

6 Exodus 1:15-21

7 **John Greenleaf Whittier,** *Dear Lord and Father of mankind.*

8 Genesis 27:41-46.

9 Genesis 32:10.

10 Genesis 12:8; 13:3-4.

11 Consider Deuteronomy 4:9; 6:4-7; Proverbs 22:6.

12 **Amelia Matilda Hull.**

13 I am using the term 'heart' in the colloquial sense, as the seat of the emotions.

14 **Frances Ridley Havergal,** *Take my life.*

15 John 14:6.

Wrestling with God

Genesis 32:22-32

It was with a mixture of wonder, joy and trepidation that Jacob completed the five hundred mile journey from Beersheba to Haran, way up in Mesopotamia. He had left home primarily to escape the wrath of his brother but, since his experience at Bethel, the task of finding a godly wife from amongst his distant relatives became his prime concern. Mere religious convictions had flowered into spiritual certainty and having defended his character even prior to his first encounter with Christ, we shall find it needs no defence in this chapter.

Twenty years of training

It is not our purpose to unravel the complicated web of intrigue into which he innocently and unwittingly stepped when he finally arrived at Uncle Laban's but, throughout his twenty year sojourn in Padan-Aram,[1] suffice it to say that Jacob conducted himself with remarkable constraint, integrity and generosity.

His supernatural change of character is all the more notable, considering the fact that, in Laban, he was constantly confronted with the brazen double-dealing of perhaps the most self-seeking, sanctimonious hypocrite the Old Testament has to offer. That having been said, it was a wonderful period of training for Jacob, away from the restrictive environment and claustrophobic atmosphere of home. Anyone that God intends to use, let alone as mightily as God intended to use Jacob, would inevitably at some time have to be removed from a weak father, a dominant mother and a worldly brother! Jacob's exile was a wonderful preparation for his return to the Promised Land and the founding of the nation.

When the Lord finally commanded him to return after those twenty years, he did so with eleven of the twelve sons, whose destiny it was to be the fathers of the tribes of Israel. God had prospered him in material terms as well, so that it was a large party of family, servants and livestock that finally entered the land their descendants would possess.

Laban had chased Jacob all the way to the hill country of Gilead in order to force him to return but, in a dream, God warned him not to interfere. From this point on, we hear no more about that branch of the family in Mesopotamia. They disappear from history entirely, no doubt intermingling with the local tribes and losing their godly heritage and distinctive identity for ever. All the concentration now is on the Promised Land and the beginning of the fulfilment of all the wonderful promises that have repeatedly been made to the patriarchs.[2]

Earnest prayer and wise precautions

That eventful twenty year interlude behind him, Jacob's thoughts now turn to the uncertain reception that awaits him. We can well imagine his emotions as he prepares to cross once more into the Promised Land. He is ninety-seven years old, and although, according to the measure of those days, still in his prime, he knew that the time had at last arrived for him to assume his full patriarchal responsibilities. Yet he had no idea what lay ahead.

His mother, you may recall, had promised to summon him as soon as Esau's anger had cooled but, as far as we know, there had been no word. Were his parents still alive? Was his brother still nursing his grievance and plotting revenge? Perhaps in order to avoid any confrontation, he enters Canaan by an alternative route, travelling southwards along the east bank of the River Jordan. Then, just as the angels of God bid him farewell at Bethel, they welcome him back at Mahanaim. 'Jacob also went on his way, and the angels of God met him. When Jacob saw them, he said, "This is the camp of God!" So he named that place Mahanaim [two camps]' (Genesis 32:1-2). Despite that divine reassurance, we soon read that he is filled with 'great fear and distress' (Genesis 32:7). A reconnaissance party has returned with the disconcerting news that Esau is on the march towards him with a force of four hundred men! As soon as they were sighted, the men came back to report.

Most of Genesis 32 is taken up with Jacob's practical arrangements to protect his people and to pacify his brother. Once, Jacob would have relied entirely on his own resources and natural cunning to see him through, but now he casts himself on God's mercy in the beautiful prayer recorded in verses 9-12. 'Then Jacob prayed, "O God of my father Abraham, God of my father Isaac, O LORD, who said to me, 'Go back to your country and your relatives, and I will make you prosper,' I am unworthy of all the kindness and faithfulness you have shown your servant. I had only my staff when I crossed this Jordan, but now I have become two groups. Save me, I pray, from the hand of my brother Esau, for I am afraid he will come and attack me, and also the mothers with their children. But you have said, 'I will surely make you prosper and will make your descendants like the sand of the sea, which cannot be counted.'"' Reverently and humbly, Jacob reminds the Lord of his provision in the past and promises for the future. It is the prayer of a mature believer and a model for any child of God in time of distress.

It is quite incredible to me when people write as they do about Jacob. How on earth do they imagine that such a terrible man as they make him out to be could suddenly utter a prayer like this? I admire Jacob's combined response of earnest prayer and wise precaution. We are rarely called simply to pray; there is usually some action that the Lord wants us to take as well.

Alone with God

At nightfall he conducts his beloved wives and sons, in whom the future of the nation resides, together with all his possessions, across the ford of the River Jabbok, a tributary that flows westward into the Jordan, about twenty miles north of the Dead Sea. He himself returns to the north bank and we read in verse 24, 'So Jacob was left alone.'

Why did he do that? Why did he put the river between himself and all he held most dear in the world? Did he know he was going to meet with God? Oh, yes! But he had not the slightest inkling of the dramatic encounter the Lord had in store for him. Jacob simply had an overwhelming desire to pray, and for that he had learnt, as have countless saints ever since, he needed to get on his own. Have you yet discovered the truth that it is alone with our God that we learn the greatest lessons and enjoy the sweetest experiences that are on offer to the earthbound believer? If Jesus himself needed to retire to 'a solitary place'[3] for communion with his Father, how much more do we?

How many of us look for complex diagnoses to account for our spiritual coldness, when all the time we are neglecting the basics. We need perhaps to spend less time with other people, so we can spend more time with God; less time with other things, so we can spend more time in prayer. It is a question of priorities, but one that is too vital for any of us to leave unanswered.

Jacob no doubt sensed that the greatest crisis of his life was upon him, but he little guessed, as his eyes strained to pierce the darkness, that he had entered upon the second of the two most significant nights of his life. Even less could he have imagined that he was about to be granted another theophany, indeed perhaps the strangest and most intimate theophany ever to be granted to anyone.

As we have implied, it seems clear that Jacob intended to spend the night in solitary prayer. Have you ever felt the need to do that? When Israel fought Amalek, Moses grew tired in prayer long before Joshua grew tired in battle.[4] True intercessory prayer is draining both emotionally and physically but there are seasons in the life of every true believer that demand a special commitment to it.

Jacob begins to pray. It is plain from the outset that he is in agony of soul. Despite his location in the hills of Gilead, there is no balm for his soul.[5] He receives no support, no help; it does not seem as though God is interested. All kinds of doubts are sown by the evil one at such a time. Gradually, as he pleads, he begins to sense the presence of God. But that brings no relief, for it feels as though God is refusing him. Jacob redoubles his efforts, he must convince the Lord, he must change his mind. Maybe, at this early stage of his prayer during that night, he was more concerned about mere physical protection than the fulfilment of the divine promises. Here was Jacob on the very threshold of the Promised Land, about to enter upon his destiny in all its fulness, and yet his heart and mind are filled with the fear of man. He is crying out to the Lord for immediate protection and the Lord is saying, 'Jacob, why are you more concerned about physical safety than the fulfilment of the spiritual promises I have made you?'

I cannot prove that this was happening, but it seems not unlikely.

Certainly most evangelical prayer meetings give the appearance of caring more for man's well-being than God's glory, more for physical ailments than spiritual ills and more for immediate needs than strategic goals. We need continually to remind ourselves of Jesus' words in the Sermon on the Mount, 'Seek first his kingdom and his righteousness, and all these things will be given to you as well' (Matthew 6:33). The Lord will never wholeheartedly respond to those of his people who are more preoccupied with their own needs than the needs of his kingdom.

Desperate for blessing

Then the wrestling in prayer becomes more and more real until, to his utter astonishment, Jacob discovers that it has *become* real and his uplifted arms are grappling with the Angel of the Lord. 'So Jacob was left alone, and a man wrestled with him till daybreak' (Genesis 32:24). I love the prophet Hosea's illuminating commentary on Jacob at this point. He says, 'In the womb he grasped his brother's heel; as a man he struggled with God. He struggled with the angel and overcame him; he wept and begged for his favour' (Hosea 12:3-4). As if the account in Genesis 32 were not sensational enough, Hosea's prophetic insight raises the scene to new heights of dramatic intensity.

Hosea points out that, just as Jacob grabbed the heel of his brother Esau at birth, so he held on to the Son of God at Peniel. Why does the prophet juxtapose these two facts? The reason is obvious! I know that God's love for Jacob was all of grace, and that the apostle Paul cites it as an example of God's sovereign and ultimately inexplicable choice,[6] but the more I study Jacob the more I can appreciate something of why God loved him so much. No one, but no one, wanted to be the recipient of God's greatest blessings more than Jacob. *Even prior to his birth,* he was so desperate at the thought of missing out that he clung to his brother's heel. 'Jacob at Peniel,' says the prophet Hosea, 'is behaving fully in character.' He was always utterly determined to receive the choicest of God's gifts and he was not going to allow anything, or anyone, to stand in his way.

That is why, to less spiritually intense people, some of Jacob's actions look totally unscrupulous. We need to take account of this desperate desire for God's blessing, bearing in mind that from infancy his mother has constantly told him it was his due. Ask yourself, when will you be able to wrestle with God like Jacob at Peniel? The answer is simple: when you want the blessing of God and the fulfilment of his promises in your life more than life itself. If that sets the standard too high for you, so be it. That is precisely why the vast majority of God's people do not enjoy more than a small proportion of the divine resources available to them. I must confess, the more deeply I consider Jacob, the more I want to be like him. Of all the patriarchs, he stands out as a model for the Christian who longs, above everything else, for communion with God.

Jesus said, 'Whoever wants to save his life will lose it, but whoever loses his life for me and for the gospel will save it' (Mark 8:35). Am I prepared to lose my life for Christ? Am I prepared to say, 'Lord, whatever it takes! My only desire is to serve you and be of use to you.' Most of us are full of excuses, looking after ourselves and content with a modicum of blessing. Jacob's hunger for the Lord bears no relation to the faint and intermittent hankering of the average believer. Yet it need not be so.

What is the point of an unconsecrated life, where Christianity is just a bolt-on extra? We bolt it on for five minutes in the morning when we flick through the Word of God and we bolt it on again for a couple of hours or so on a Sunday! What is the point of that? It is mere existence, whereas Christ promises abundant life to those who are prepared to give themselves entirely to him.

All this calls for no thoughtless wave of enthusiasm. We have to count the cost and see if we are really willing to pay it. And there is no better place in Scripture to help us do that than the famous passage before us.

When God seems against us

This is especially for you if, like Jacob, you are at a critical juncture in your life and the future fills you with a certain fear and foreboding. 'So Jacob was left alone. And a man wrestled with him till daybreak.' It seems, perhaps, as though God himself has ambushed you and is against you. Well, good! He must love you very much to spend such energy opposing you until your selfish will submits to his. Can you not see that this grim and deadly struggle is designed to break whatever remnants of pride remain and render your spirit sweet and docile and sensitive to the Saviour's slightest whisper? Jacob had undergone a long preparation for the moment he would enter the Promised Land and become an active partner in the outworking of his destiny. Here, at Peniel, he passes through God's finishing school.

Moses says, 'The Lord is a warrior' (Exodus 15:3), and, in a sense, he is always wrestling with us, as we continually attempt to assert our own wills. It may be at work, in our families or even in the church. It happens in all sorts of different contexts, as we try to funnel things along in the direction we mistakenly believe to be right. In such situations, God is wrestling with us, as he seeks to conform our will to his.

Paradoxically, however, it is just when we become aware of our wilfulness and seek to concede, that the conflict suddenly becomes more real, intense and personal. The Lord wants to know how serious we are, how far we are prepared to go, how determined we are to please him, how desperate to receive his blessing.

'So Jacob was left alone. And a man wrestled with him till daybreak.' How easy for Jacob to have given up, and said, 'Look, it's hopeless! Here I am trying to pray and even God is against me! Here I am seeking his help and wanting to please him and he comes and attacks me!' So many believers despair when this happens and are spiritually defeated. We must never give in, *especially* when it appears that God is against us. Great rewards await those who hold on for what seems like grim death.

Believers who seriously want to be used by the Lord will have their resolve tested. It is easy to misinterpret what is happening and to become completely discouraged. Many find that as soon as they attempt to deepen their commitment to Christ, everything in their life that *can* go wrong *does*! The tragic result is that then they turn away, fail to enter into their spiritual inheritance, and wander back into the desert.

But Jacob does not misinterpret what is happening. This godly man sees his title to the Promised Land too clearly and, despite this fearful experience, he knows that God intends him to have it. He has come to that place spiritually where, along with Job, he can say, 'Though he slay me, yet will I hope in him' (Job 13:15).

Hanging on

'So Jacob was left alone, and a man wrestled with him till daybreak. When the man saw that he could not overpower him, he touched the socket of Jacob's hip so that his hip was wrenched as he wrestled with the man' (Genesis 32:24-25). The struggle is real. It goes on for hours, but all at once this mysterious Stranger, this 'Traveller unknown',[7] reveals his power. A single touch cripples Jacob's efforts and brings him quickly to an end of himself.

Thank God for that kind of divine touch. We often thank God for a healing touch, when is the last time you thanked him for a crippling touch? Yet, for Jacob, it was the beginning of the fulfilment of all that God had for him. Thank God for those moments when we suddenly realise just how weak and helpless we are and all our proud ideas and fancy schemes fall to the ground; provided, that is, that we do not fall to the ground with them.

It is so sad when believers have been taught by the grace of God to despair of themselves, only to wallow in self-pity and conclude that they are 'useless'. They are some of the most morbid, introspective and hopeless cases imaginable, their profession of uselessness proving to be a self-fulfilling prophecy. Jacob does not fall into this trap; he realises that there has to be more. Such a humbling experience as this crippling touch must lead to despair unless we go on to understand, by faith, that Christ's 'power is made perfect in weakness' (2 Corinthians 12:9). Events now take a surprising turn.

'Then the man said, "Let me go, for it is daybreak." But Jacob replied, "I will not let you go unless you bless me"' (Genesis 32:26). Far from giving up, falling to the ground, playing dead and hoping his adversary will depart, though he can no longer fight, he clings on in utter desperation. It is as though he is saying,

'Other refuge have I none;
Hangs my helpless soul on Thee;
Leave, ah! Leave me not alone,
Still support and comfort me.'[8]

Jacob now knows what he has to do. He is greatly excited. This is the most critical moment in his spiritual experience. If he fails now he might be left in despair for the rest of his life. He could not run after the One who has crippled him, so he must hang on in desperation. We need to be brought to the point where we simply cling to the Lord Jesus Christ and lean all our weight on him.

It was hard for Jacob; it is especially hard for those who have considerable natural abilities. It is not our weakness but our strength that lies in the way of blessing. When Jacob was strong, the Son of God attacked him and he was immediately on the defensive. Now he is weak, he takes the initiative and clings on for all he is worth. How simple and yet how profound are the lessons to be learned here.

The Lord is overjoyed with Jacob's insistence on being blessed by him. He has always loved him, but never more than now. Immediately, there comes the glorious reward of grace: 'The man asked him, "What is your name?" "Jacob," he answered.' 'Jacob' — 'the one who grasps the heel' or 'the supplanter', as it came to be understood. 'Then the man said, "Your name will no longer be Jacob, but Israel, because you have struggled with God and with men and have overcome"' (Genesis 32:27-28).

The Lord Jesus Christ says to him, 'You are no "supplanter". You are the one I *chose* to love, the one who will be the father of a *nation* I have *chosen* to love. From now on, you will be called "he struggles with God" (Israel), for you have done so, and have overcome.' Overcome? Had he not lost the contest? In natural terms, of course, he had; how could anyone defeat God? Jacob's victory was in spiritual terms. God himself is unable to withstand the power of faith in his own promises.

The apostle Paul knew this secret: 'When I am weak, then I am strong' (2 Corinthians 12:10). It is a mystery to the world, but an open secret to believers who have grasped it. Have you experienced for yourself the true meaning of 'Israel'? Have you discovered how to wrestle with God and prevail? Jacob's change of name marks the moment when the time of preparation for the new nation gives way to the time of fulfilment.

Greatly emboldened by the Stranger's words and characteristically wishing to pursue to its limit such a unique opportunity for further revelation, Jacob says, 'Please tell me *your* name' (verse 29). For hours he has ventured everything on the conviction that he is struggling with the Lord himself. It is not as though he is ignorant of the Man's identity, nor even that he is seeking confirmation. With great daring he wants to be told more about God's nature than has ever yet been revealed. How typical of Jacob, and how admirable! What follows is no rebuke, it is merely that the request exceeds what the Lord, at this time, is prepared to reveal.[9] He counters with, 'Why do you ask my name?' In other words, 'Jacob, you know who I am, and that is enough.' It is thrilling to realise that we know far more of the Saviour's name than ever Jacob did on earth.

Limping into the Promised Land

'Then he blessed him there' (verse 29). Presumably, the substance of the blessing was the same as we have encountered time and again as we have looked at these theophanies. How good of God constantly to repeat his precious promises to us. 'He knows how we are formed, he remembers that we are dust' (Psalm 103:14).

The Son of God blessed him 'there', the very place of trial, weakness and despair became the place of blessing, as is so often the case.

'Ye fearful saints fresh courage take,
The clouds ye so much dread,
Are big with mercy, and shall break
In blessings on your head.'[10]

'So Jacob called the place Peniel, saying, "It is because I saw God face to face, and yet my life was spared"' (Genesis 32:30). The very name 'Peniel', which means 'face of God', celebrates not Jacob's victory but God's mercy. He had had a uniquely close encounter with the Son of God and survived. He knows it is all of grace.

Then we read, 'The sun rose above him as he passed Peniel' (verse 31). A new day of light and hope was dawning after the darkness of that dreadful night. 'The path of the righteous is like the first gleam of dawn, shining ever brighter till the full light of day' (Proverbs 4:18).

'The sun rose above him as he passed Peniel, and he was limping because of his hip.' Well, as Jesus says, 'It is better for you to enter life crippled than to have two feet and be thrown into hell' (Mark 9:45). It is better to limp into the Promised Land than to leap back into some kind of spiritual wilderness.

Besides, I think Jacob was pleased to limp! It assured him in the morning that it had not all just been a dream, and it reminded him for the rest of his life that the Lord had *allowed* him to prevail. I can imagine people saying to him, 'Jacob, how did you get that limp?' Do you not think he would have loved to have been asked that? 'Well,' says Jacob, 'I was wrestling with God!' And from then on, if anyone opposed him, he would be able to say, with more literal truth than the apostle, 'Let no one cause me trouble, for I bear on my body the marks of Jesus' (Galatians 6:17).

It all comes down to this: how much do we really want God's blessing? Does not Jacob's desperate struggle reveal our faint and sporadic desires to be more than a little half-hearted? Do you see what is required? We need spiritual wisdom to understand the Lord's dealings with us and then equal courage and stamina to gain the greatest blessings he longs to bestow. All these necessary graces God will give to those who ask him.

Isaiah, the prophet, complained to his God, 'No one calls on your name or strives to lay hold of you' (Isaiah 64:7). The Lord Jesus declared, 'The kingdom of heaven has been forcefully advancing and forceful men lay hold of it' (Matthew 11:12). They lay hold of it with all their being. True spirituality is a matter of neither sport nor show. It is not for the fainthearted. Nonetheless, its joys and rewards are beyond the power of human telling.

Notes

1 Genesis 31:38.

2 The account of Jacob's stay in Haran and his tumultuous return journey is to be found in Genesis 29-31.

3 Matthew 14:13; Mark 1:35.

4 Exodus 17:8-16.

5 Jeremiah 8:22.

6 Romans 9:10-16.

7 **Charles Wesley's** great hymn, *Come, O thou Traveller unknown*, is a sermon all of its own on this passage.

8 **Charles Wesley,** *Jesu, Lover of my soul.*

9 The Lord finally revealed his name to Moses in the theophany at the burning bush. See Exodus 3:13-15; 6:2-3.

10 **William Cowper,** *God moves in a mysterious way.*

Reformation in the family

Genesis 35:1-15

According to our strict definition of the term, we have looked at all but one of the theophanies in the Book of Genesis. In this chapter we shall complete the survey, with the Lord's final appearance to Jacob.[1] Genesis 35 not only sees the end of the theophanies, but the end of an era. Chapter 36 marks this with lists of genealogies and, from chapter 37 on, Joseph is the hero in what is very clearly a totally new section of the book.

Two significant changes should be noted. Unlike Abraham, Isaac and Jacob, Joseph is not in the Messianic line and that is probably the principal reason why he does not receive a theophany. Also, the covenant people as a whole, by virtue of Jacob's twelve sons, now have many fathers. The nation has been founded and the Son of God decides that he need no longer reveal himself on earth until the destiny of Israel is once again entrusted to just one man, with the raising up of Moses. But that is another story, outside the scope of this book.

This third, last and least well-known theophany granted to Jacob actually made the most enduring impression upon him. When he lay on his deathbed in Egypt many years later, it was not the stairway to heaven that he recalled, nor did even his wrestling with the Saviour at Peniel come to mind. No, it was this final and most gracious of all appearances that filled his heart with wonder and with gratitude.[2] Nor should we be surprised at this for, amazing though it may seem, even after he had 'overcome' the Lord at Peniel and received his new name of Israel, he contrived to get himself and the fledgling nation into the most appalling mess!

A disastrous move

Jacob was delighted to discover that Esau bore him no grudge after their twenty-year separation, but he was right to refuse his invitation to stay with his brother's people down in Seir. Freshly envisioned as he was from having seen God 'face to face' at Peniel, he knew that he had to remain in the Promised Land and that his family must now retain its distinct identity.

Furthermore, he was probably not wrong in returning across the River Jabbok to a place called Succoth where he had noticed there was fine pasture for his people and his herds to recover their strength. They must all have been physically and emotionally exhausted after the long flight from Laban and the fearful prospect of a hostile Esau waiting for them. It was good for there to be this time for recuperation and reflection.[3]

The key mistake he made occurs at the end of chapter 33. 'After Jacob came from Padan Aram, he arrived safely at the city of Shechem in Canaan and camped within sight of the city. For a hundred pieces of silver, he bought from the sons of Hamor, the father of Shechem, the plot of ground where he pitched his tent. There he set up an altar and called it El Elohe Israel [God is the God of Israel]' (Genesis 33:18-20). As ever, Jacob's zeal far outstripped his discretion.

The result of that disastrous move across the River Jordan to Shechem was rape, mass murder, shame and the imminent destruction of God's chosen people. Genesis 34 records the defiling of Jacob's daughter, Dinah, and the subsequent, dreadful revenge of Jacob's sons upon the men of Shechem. None of the men involved emerge with any credit from the sickening events related here. We can only marvel at the honesty of Moses in including this damning indictment of the fathers of the tribes of Israel in his inspired history and, most of all, the amazing grace God displayed in not discarding them.

A flavour of the ghastly situation, including the relationship that obtained between Jacob and his sons, is perfectly conveyed in the last couple of verses of the chapter: 'Then Jacob said to Simeon and Levi, "You have brought trouble on me by making me a stench to the Canaanites and Perizzites, the people living in this land. We are few in number, and if they join forces against me and attack me, I and my household will be destroyed." But they replied, "Should he have treated our sister like a prostitute?"' That is the dramatic ending of Genesis 34. Just that final exchange discloses an astonishing catalogue of blatant sin. Jacob seems only concerned about himself, utterly indifferent to the evils committed by his sons and more worried about upsetting the Canaanites than the Lord. Little wonder that his sons appear insolent, violent and lawless.

We are probably ten years down the line from that tremendous night when Jacob wrestled with, and overcame, the Son of God at Peniel, but even so, how could things have been reduced to this, the family of God's choice polluting the land he has chosen for them, the family itself riven apart by a careless father and his rebellious sons? It comes as a dreadful shock and seems almost to defy belief. Everything had gone horribly wrong. Surely the salt had lost its savour and the good seed was dead before it could be sown.

This dreadful episode would eventually shake Jacob out of his appalling complacency but, initially, I suspect he was completely nonplussed at the turn events had taken. He need not have been; there was a degree of inevitability about the whole, sorry saga. Sadly, many Christian families easily get themselves into a similarly unholy mess and appear to be equally bewildered as to where, if at all, they went wrong.

A broken vow

Let us get the reasons for Jacob's family failure sorted out for a start. They all stem from the fact that Jacob did not keep the vow he had made all those years before at Bethel. Remember, he was fleeing from his brother Esau, his only belongings a staff and the clothes on his back, when the Lord first appeared to him in a dream, standing at the top of a stairway leading up to heaven.

Having received the covenant promises, the following morning 'Jacob made a vow, saying, "If [or *since*] God will be with me and will watch over me on this journey I am taking and will give me food to eat and clothes to wear so that I return safely to my father's house, then *the LORD will be my God* and this stone that I have set up as a pillar will be God's house, and of all that you give me I will give you a tenth"' (Genesis 28:20-22). Never mind the two subsidiary promises for the moment, the basic pledge had been, 'The Lord will be my God.'

A vow is a solemn matter that a believer should rarely make and never break. We make vows when we marry and, perhaps, when we are baptised. A vow is not an everyday occurrence. It certainly was not for Jacob. Solomon was to put it succinctly: 'When you make a vow to God, do not delay in fulfilling in it. He has no pleasure in fools; fulfil your vow. It is better not to make a vow than to make a vow and not fulfil it. Do not let your mouth lead you into sin' (Ecclesiastes 5:4-6). We should never make promises to one another that we do not keep. How much worse to break the most solemn of promises made to God himself! If I make a promise to God, he will keep me to it. He will say, 'I expect you to take me at *my* word, so I will take you at *your* word.'

Have you made vows in the past that you have not kept? Ask the Lord to bring them to mind, so that you might rectify matters. This passage teaches us that failure to keep a vow entails consequences. I have no doubt Jacob would have said 'Amen' to the words of Solomon, but whatever Jacob may have said or thought, and even though he set up an altar in Shechem and called it 'God is the God of Israel', it meant nothing if he was plain disobedient.

It does not matter if we believe all the right things and even profess our faith openly for all to hear; if our lives are essentially disobedient to God then it means nothing. In fact it means worse than nothing, it means we are hypocrites. One of the subsidiary promises Jacob had made in his vow was to establish a place of worship at Bethel on his return to the Promised Land. Yet although he had lived for ten years or so just fifteen miles away at Shechem, for some reason he neglected to fulfil his vow, presumably because it was far more convenient for him to build an altar and worship at home. How dangerous it is for ourselves and our families when we make our worship and Christian service a matter of convenience.

There again, if God had really been his God he would not have settled at Shechem anyway! During the time he was still working for Laban back in Padan Aram, the Lord God had explicitly commanded him to return not only to the Promised Land, but to his relatives.[4] In other words, he should have gone back to his father Isaac who was still alive and residing at Hebron.

Quite probably Jacob chose to live near Shechem for practical and sentimental reasons. In practical terms, the location provided rich pasture for his animals. But he was also doubtless well aware that Shechem was the place where the Lord had first appeared to his grandfather Abraham on entering the Promised Land.[5] Maybe Jacob thought he was treading in his grandfather's footsteps and sought the blessing where Abraham had found it.

We have already had occasion to note the dangers of sentimental guidance. Remember how it was that Isaac had taken himself off to Beer Lahai Roi, where Hagar had seen the Lord, hoping perhaps that history might repeat itself.[6] It is very dangerous to be led by sentiment. God determined, according to the apostle Paul, the 'exact places' where we should live (Acts 17:26). We can be absolutely certain when it comes to moving our home or our job location that God will clearly guide us. It need never be a matter of guesswork, nor are we to be driven by pure desire, convenience or sentiment. (For those with over-active consciences, I should perhaps add that neither are desirability and convenience to be seen as contraindications of the Lord's will!)

Spiritual laxity

Moreover, Jacob should not have *bought* the land from a Canaanite. It was one thing to buy a plot in the Promised Land in order to be buried there — that was an act of faith — but it was quite another to buy a plot of land to live in. This was an insult to God, who would eventually *give* all of Canaan to Israel. Until that time, God's people were to live in the land as 'aliens and strangers.' In the same way, we are to sit light to the world. We are not to have such a stake in it that might suggest we are not 'longing for a better country — a heavenly one', which God has prepared for us (Hebrews 11:13-16). How easy it is to become ensnared by the ideas, values and goals of a godless world.[7]

This leads us on, regrettably, to add that not only was Jacob living in the wrong place, but he was also living in the wrong way. Sadly, the poor example his own father had set while he was growing up, resulted, as it so often does, in the cycle repeating itself. He appears to have been as sinfully indulgent and tolerant concerning his sons' behaviour as King David was later to be.[8]

Amazingly, Jacob allowed his household to possess pagan idols and other religious paraphernalia. Perhaps he had become aware that Rachel had stolen Laban's household gods[9] and did not want to upset her by removing them. Once the rest of the household heard about that and saw what was acceptable, no doubt they started to collect them for themselves. After all, as Paul was fond of saying, 'A little yeast works through the whole batch of dough' (1 Corinthians 5:6; Galatians 5:9).

Jacob's spiritual laxity was further displayed in the way he permitted his family to mingle, ultimately so disastrously, with the Shechemites. Where was the supposed spiritual leader when Dinah, his daughter, was raped? You find, as you read through chapter 34, that he fades almost imperceptibly from the scene and, by default, allows his sons to plan and execute their dreadful scheme. Even the way the sons speak to their father at the end of chapter 34, tells its own story of Jacob's failings as the head of his house. Fathers who abdicate their spiritual responsibilities and allow their children to live godless lives in worldly company really have no cause to be surprised when evil results.

All this occurred because he failed to keep his vow, 'The Lord will be my God'. He thought he had kept it, but he did not appreciate how it had to be worked out in daily life. He is guilty of presumption and complacency, two of the most insidious of spiritual diseases. He imagined that because God had blessed him mightily on his return to the Promised Land, all would necessarily be well. Solomon shakes his head in grave concern: 'A little sleep, a little slumber, a little folding of the hands to rest — and poverty will come on you like a bandit and scarcity like an armed man' (Proverbs 6:10-11). 'Woe to you who are complacent in Zion', thunders the prophet Amos (Amos 6:1). It is such a common malady, but none the less serious for that. The apostle Paul frequently warned of its dangers. He told the Christians in Rome, 'The hour has come for you to wake up from your slumber, because our salvation is nearer now than when we first believed' (Romans 13:11).

The Lord allows Jacob to doze while everything falls apart in order to teach him this final great lesson of his life. But just when matters appear desperate and hopelessly out of hand, we read the opening two words of chapter 35, 'Then God...' The Lord had of course kept his commitment at Bethel perfectly. Only Jacob had failed. Yet such is God's wonderful grace that, at the precise moment that all seemed lost, he steps in.

'Then God said to Jacob, "Go up to Bethel and settle there"'. 'Settle' sounds too permanent to be a good translation here. As we have seen, it had always been the Lord's intention that Jacob should finally settle with his father in the patriarchal home at Hebron. God intended that Jacob should move to Bethel as an interim measure, to get things sorted out and to fulfil the relevant part of his vow. 'Go up to Bethel and settle [linger] there, and build an altar there to God, who appeared to you when you were fleeing from your brother Esau' (Genesis 35:1).

A divine prescription

Oh, Jacob! If only you had done the obvious thing, the promised thing, when you first arrived back in Canaan, instead of wasting, worse than wasting, those ten years or so in Shechem. Praise the Lord that he is famous for being the God of second chances; yes, and of third, fourth and fifth chances too! We are not to tempt him, but let us all express our gratitude for this aspect of his merciful nature on which we sadly depend so much.

Would you not have thought, after all the blessings showered on Jacob and the desperate mess he had made of it all, that God would have said, 'Enough!'? But he did not. Whether it be Jacob or David, Jonah or Peter, you or me, the Lord will never allow those on whom he has set his love to fall completely.

Perhaps you and your family are in a spiritual mess and can identify only too easily with that spiritual disobedience and weakness that has caused it. The good news is that there is a prescription here which, if followed, will result in restoration. The remedy is in four stages.

1 RECOGNISE THAT GOD IS TELLING YOU TO MAKE A FRESH START

'Then God said to Jacob, "Go up to Bethel and settle there, and build an altar there to God, who appeared to you when you were fleeing from your brother Esau"' (Genesis 35:1). There is no doubt that Jacob, probably paralysed by the sheer awfulness of the situation, must have gasped with relief at hearing God's voice again and being offered this lifeline. Here was an opportunity to put what had happened behind him and to start again.

The Lord is doing the same for you if he is reminding you of broken promises. Recognise what he is saying and resolve to make a fresh start. You must not slide down any further. 'Go up to Bethel', whatever that might mean for you. Be determined to return spiritually to the place where you had no resources to rely on except the promises of God; where you received a fresh vision of Jesus and were prepared to step out into the unknown, confident that he was with you.

There were no worldly attractions for Jacob at Bethel. That high rocky plateau held no lure for a wealthy cattle man. But the stirring of old memories, when spiritual choices and life itself were simpler, would prove irresistible, now that he knew that God himself had renewed the invitation. Is it the same for you?

2 ROOT OUT AND BURY EVERYTHING THAT IS UNGODLY

'So Jacob said to his household and to all who were with him, "Get rid of the foreign gods you have with you, and purify yourselves and change your clothes"' (Genesis 35:2). You can see how God was in this. Not only has Jacob suddenly come alive again and been infused with a new decisiveness not seen for years, but his rebellious family instantly, meekly and gladly obeys! On previous form, we might have expected Jacob's words to have precipitated a heated argument, or perhaps, more likely, to have been greeted with amazement and laughed to scorn. But no, we read in verse 4, 'So they gave Jacob all the foreign gods they had and the rings in their ears, and Jacob buried them under the oak at Shechem.'

Astonishing! How simple it all becomes when God is at work. Jacob would have been afraid to have commanded this before, even had he wanted to. Now all his old holy courage has returned, and the Lord immediately owns it. What we are beginning to see here is no mere outward reformation but family revival, the fruit of true repentance.

Christian fathers, do not be afraid. If God puts it in your heart to lead your family as you should, he will honour that in ways that will surprise and thrill you. 'Get rid of the foreign gods you have with you, and purify yourselves and change your clothes.' We must root out every impure, worldly and selfish motive, any aims and ambitions that, as a family we put idolatrously before seeking and serving the Lord. How wonderful it is when the Holy Spirit washes us clean again and every family member puts on the new clothes of 'compassion, kindness, humility, gentleness and patience' (Colossians 3:12). You do not believe it is possible? Jacob would have said the same before the Lord spoke to him.

I love to picture to myself the whole household standing round with joyful resolution as Jacob buried all these religious trinkets and all the paraphernalia of paganism under the oak at Shechem. The spiritual application is obvious. We are to bury all the remnants of the old life, whatever they may be. So let us bury them deep, pound down the earth on top of them and never return to the site. May the Holy Spirit move us to pray,

The dearest idol I have known,
Whate'er that idol be,
Help me to tear it from Thy throne,
And worship only Thee.[10]

I suppose, from a human point of view, everyone was so shocked at the excess to which they had attained, that it had been rather like a cold douche of water, bringing them all to their senses. Thank God if he has so dealt with you; but thank God even more if he has achieved the same effect by gentler means! Do not tempt him into taking such drastic action in the life of your family that you are just shocked into submission and stunned into acceptance of God's will. Here is an example for us that we should avoid as well as a way out that we should emulate.

3 REMOVE YOURSELF FROM ALL WORLDLY AND UNHELPFUL ASSOCIATIONS

'Then come, let us *go* . . .' (Genesis 35:3). Jacob had to remove his family from the baneful influence of the Shechemites. He should never have been there in the first place. The necessity of a right separation between the people of God and the world is a constant biblical theme from Genesis to Revelation.[11]

The dangers of ignoring this principle are repeatedly illustrated. Remember how Lot began by pitching his tents 'near Sodom' (Genesis 13:12), but ended up within its gates. Jacob, thankfully, was woken up to his spiritual peril and responsibilities just in time. It is as though he heard the words of the Holy Spirit through the prophet Micah, 'Get up, go away! For this is not your resting place, because it is defiled, it is ruined, beyond all remedy' (Micah 2:10).

Spiritually speaking, this applies to our relationships and associations, the things we like to get involved in. Just as we must root out and bury all the ungodly attitudes and motives that destroy our testimony and so easily poison our family life, so we must also distance ourselves from any external influences that so easily contaminate and drag us down. Wherever we deliberately go, whatever we deliberately look at, listen to or do that we sense is spiritually harmful, must be abandoned. Such things will not leave you; you have to leave them. 'Then come, let us go', says Jacob. And about time too!

4 RE-ESTABLISH TRUE WORSHIP

'Jacob and all the people with him came to Luz (that is, Bethel) in the land of Canaan. There he built an altar, and he called the place El Bethel, because it was there that God revealed himself to him when he was fleeing from his brother' (Genesis 35:6-7).

What did Jacob say to his family when he had them all assembled at Bethel? They would have looked about somewhat quizzically at their strange surroundings in that rocky valley. Jacob's eyes would have been fixed on the stone he had so reverently erected thirty years or so before. Suddenly, his reverie is broken. 'Father, why have you brought us here?' For Jacob, it is time for soul-searching, time perhaps for confession. I imagine him saying, 'Well, I think I told you years ago, although I have not told you often enough, what God did for me here at Bethel. I saw a stairway linking earth and heaven, and the Lord standing at the top. He confirmed to me my destiny and promised he would always watch over me and never leave me and would bring me back to this land. That experience utterly changed me overnight. The next morning I made a vow. I promised that he would be my God and that, when he brought me back, this stone that I set up would become God's house.'[12]

And they would say, 'Father, why have you waited all this time?' To which he would reply, 'I have no excuse, no excuse at all. I should have done it years ago. It would have spared us all the misery, the heartache and the sin that we have fallen into in these past years. I accept full responsibility for all that has taken place. I have asked for the forgiveness of my God, and now I ask for yours.'

You may fairly comment that this speech is the product of mere speculation, but it is difficult to believe that what actually occurred was very different. What a scene it must have been! How the tears must have flowed!

It must have been very humbling for Jacob, but he would have felt strangely better and stronger for his admission of guilt and acceptance of responsibility. Without a doubt, his confession and repentance were echoed in the hearts, words and actions of them all. Far from despising him, his family surely felt a strong surge of love for him, discovering a new respect and a new sense of loyalty towards him. So at last the altar was built and the chosen family worshipped once more together, at Bethel, the house of God.

I know there are many Christian fathers who would do well to follow this biblical prescription for restoring the family. You know, it is never too late. The youngest of Jacob's children were by now in their late teens. Some fathers are concerned that, whatever else might be achieved, their families would never agree to the establishing of family worship. They say, 'I've left it too late; I don't think I can do it now. We just have to pray privately to God that our children will somehow come back and find the Lord.' But, again, I would say, it is never too late. Do not be afraid to try. In my experience, there are many wives and children who are simply longing for the husband and father to take the spiritual lead in the home. The results may be far, far greater and more blessed than you could ever imagine. They certainly were for Jacob.

One thing is sure, a special protection will be granted to all those who are prepared to embark on such a project. The potential consequences of the whole of Jacob's household resorting to Bethel for worship were so tremendous that the Lord pulled out all the stops to ensure their safe passage. 'Then they set out, and the terror of God fell upon the towns all around them so that no-one pursued them' (Genesis 35:5). Despite the repugnance and hostility all the Canaanite tribes must have felt at this point towards Jacob and his people, they are all supernaturally restrained. No-one is allowed to touch God's anointed ones when they seek to do his will. 'When a man's ways are pleasing to the Lord, he makes even his enemies live at peace with him' (Proverbs 16:7). Seek to restore your family to the glory of God and the forces of heaven will be mobilised to assist!

The final appearance

Now, at last, we come to the theophany itself! We have left it so late because we could not possibly have appreciated what it meant to Jacob without considering all that preceded it. I do not suppose that Jacob believed for a moment that the Lord would ever condescend to appear to him again after all his wicked unfaithfulness. Yet that is the nature of the Son of God. We are about to glance at not only Jacob's last, true theophany, but the last theophany granted to the founding fathers of the nation and the last theophany in the Book of Genesis. This time, the Lord does not appear at the top of a stairway in a dream, nor does he come violently upon him as at Peniel. Instead, he stands beside the one he loves and talks with him. No wonder Jacob recalls *this*, the most precious of all three appearances, on his deathbed. No wonder he repeats the words he heard fall from those sacred lips almost verbatim.

But notice the introduction. 'After Jacob returned from Padan-Aram, God appeared to him again and blessed him' (Genesis 35:9). It is as though the great Director has cried, 'Cut!' and ordered that the whole story be retold from Jacob's entry into the Promised Land ten years previously. The slate has been wiped clean. It is as though the whole shameful episode never happened! What a vivid illustration of a glorious truth. 'I, even I, am he who blots out your transgressions, for my own sake, and remembers your sins no more' (Isaiah 43:25).

Verse 10 confirms the impression: 'God said to him, "Your name is Jacob, but you will no longer be called Jacob; your name will be Israel." So he named him Israel.' Had not the Lord changed his name ten years before at Peniel?[13] Yes, but the renaming is repeated nonetheless. It is done without rebuke, indeed without comment, but the message is unmistakably powerful. The Lord is saying to Jacob, 'Remember! And this time, Israel, be what you are!' We all need the same message. The Lord wants us to progress, not constantly to find ourselves at the starting-line.

I think of the words of the apostle Paul, 'As a prisoner for the Lord, then, I urge you to live a life worthy of the calling you have received' (Ephesians 4:1). From this moment on, Jacob finally does. 'And God said to him, "I am God Almighty; be fruitful and increase in number. A nation and a community of nations will come from you, and kings will come from your body. The land I gave to Abraham and Isaac I also give to you, and I will give this land to your descendants after you"' (Genesis 35:11-12). God renews those old, familiar, and yet ever-staggering promises. May all the old, familiar and even more wonderful promises of the gospel be renewed in us as well.

'Then God went up from him at the place where he had *talked* with him. Jacob set up a stone pillar at the place where God had *talked* with him, and he poured out a drink offering on it; he also poured oil on it. Jacob called the place where God had *talked* with him Bethel' (Genesis 35:13-15). Three times in those final three verses it is noted that God Almighty *talked* with a man. As the Lord disappears from Jacob's sight for the last time it is good to be reminded of the abiding legacy of these theophanies. What was seen was for the moment and faded away, but what was heard was for all time and eternity.

Notes

1 I do not regard Genesis 46:2-4 as a true theophany. There is no conclusive evidence that the Lord *appeared* to Jacob. The word translated 'vision' could be better translated here 'revelation'. The same is true in 1 Samuel 3:15. It is obvious from the account that Samuel did

not see who was speaking to him. Compare the last verse of the same chapter.

2 Genesis 48:3-4. The wording of verse 4 indicates it was his third rather than his first theophany that he had in mind.

3 Genesis 33:1-17.

4 Genesis 31:3.

5 Genesis 12:6-7. See Chapter 3.

6 See Chapter 9.

7 1 John 2:15-17 is a classic statement on the Christian's attitude to the world.

8 1 Kings 1:6 gives us the general idea of David's parenting policy.

9 Genesis 31:19, 30-35.

10 William Cowper, 'O for a closer walk with God'.

11 Perhaps the most trenchant New Testament statement of the principle is to be found in 2 Corinthians 6:14-18.

12 The account is found in Genesis 28:10-22. See Chapter 10.

13 Genesis 32:27-28.

Also from Day One

The Ten Commandments for today

Brian H. Edwards

Large format paperback
288 pages **£8.99**

At a time when the nation's morality is in alarming decline, it is surprising that so little has been written on the Ten Commandments. Brian Edwards gives us a modern commentary, carefully uncovering their true meaning and incisively applying them to our contemporary society. Probably never in the history of western civilisation have the Ten Commandments been more neglected and therefore more relevant than today.

With more than 30 years in a pastoral and preaching ministry, **Brian Edwards** has authored a number of books including *God's Outlaw*, a biography of William Tyndale, and the study of Biblical authority, *Nothing but the truth*. He also wrote the popular *In Conversation* series published by Day One, and co- authored with his wife Barbara the marriage preparation course, *No Longer Two.*

ISBN 0 902548 69 7

The Beatitudes for Today

John Blanchard

Large format paperback
263 pages **£7.95**

In his foreword, Eric J. Alexander writes, "this book fills a significant gap in contemporary Christian writing. Although the past thirty years have seen the publication of several excellent volumes on the Sermon on the Mount, we have lacked a full-length treatment of the Beatitudes. The Christian world has been deeply indebted to John Blanchard for his preaching and writing ministry over many years. Both are characterised by an absolute faithfulness to the text of Scripture, a deep concern to apply God's Word to today's world, and a God-given insight into the implications of biblical truth."

John Blanchard is an internationally known British Evangelist and Bible teacher, who has written a number of best-selling books including *Ultimate Questions, Right with God, Pop Goes the Gospel* and *Whatever Happened to Hell?*

ISBN 0 902548 67 0

For further information about other Day One titles, call or write to us:

01372 728 300

In Europe: ++ 44 1372 728 300

In North America: 011 44 1372 728 300

Day One No. 3 Epsom Business Park Kiln Lane Epsom Surrey KT17 1JF England

e-mail address: ldos.dayone@ukonline.co.uk